# COMPUTER P<br>IN FORTRAN

Arthur Radford became involved in computing after working as a radar instructor in the RAF. He has wide experience in commercial programming, including preparing computer manuals for STC and working as a systems programmer with Boeing Commercial Airplane Division in America. He began lecturing at Leicester Polytechnic and is now Senior Lecturer in the Department of Computer Studies and Mathematics at Bristol Polytechnic.

TEACH YOURSELF BOOKS

# COMPUTER PROGRAMMING IN FORTRAN

Arthur S. Radford

TEACH YOURSELF BOOKS

Hodder and Stoughton

*First published 1983*

British Library Cataloguing in Publication Data

Radford, Arthur S.
Computer programming in FORTRAN.—
(Teach yourself books)
1. FORTRAN (Computer program language)
I. Title
001.64′24    QA76.73.F25

ISBN 0 340 27587 1

*Printed and bound in Great Britain*
*for Hodder and Stoughton Educational,*
*a division of Hodder and Stoughton Ltd,*
*Mill Road, Dunton Green, Sevenoaks, Kent,*
*by Richard Clay (The Chaucer Press) Ltd, Bungay, Suffolk*
*Phototypeset by Wyvern Typesetting Ltd, Bristol*

# Contents

# Preface

There can be no doubt about it, the computer is here to stay. For less than £50 ($100) you can walk into a High Street store and walk out five minutes later with a computer in your briefcase or handbag. Some will even fit your breast pocket. And these are not toys; they are real computers, capable of doing a real job of work. Not quite so flexible, perhaps, and much slower in action than the large 'mainframe' machines of industry and commerce, but none the less real for that and working on exactly the same basic principles.

It is not difficult for a person of average intelligence and some interest in problem-solving to learn to program a computer, of whatever type, using one of the many high-level programming languages that are now available. The purpose of this book is to provide a brief course on the more important features of the ever popular FORTRAN language in its latest standard version, FORTRAN 77. No prior knowledge of computers is needed, but it will help if you have some slight acquaintance with arithmetic and algebra. The normal secondary school leaving certificate level – GCE 'O' or CSE in the UK – should be quite adequate.

The coverage is neither rigorous nor complete; such claims would be impertinent in a book of this size and price. Even so, it does introduce all the main features of FORTRAN 77, and will enable the reader to write perfectly good programs after only a short study period. It will help enormously if you have access to a computer with a FORTRAN 77 system, but if you do not you can still get a very good idea of what it is all about by reading this book.

FORTRAN 77 is the latest in a series of FORTRAN definitions, and differs in many respects from its immediate predecessor, FORTRAN 66 (or FORTRAN IV). Realising that, even after five years, there are still many users of FORTRAN 66, I have given a brief summary, in Appendix B, of the important differences between the languages. In so far as the omissions are concerned, the ENTRY and alternate RETURN features have been missed out deliberately. There is no real need for them, except that seen by programmers who have become dependent on similar, previously available non-standard features. Both are easily implemented, if desperately needed, using other language features. The ENQUIRE statement is not dealt with, since it is rather complex for the beginning programmer. Indeed, it was with some trepidation that the OPEN statement was included, but it is difficult, if not impossible, to do any file handling without it, and the concepts involved are quite important. ASSIGN and the assigned GO TO are now so rarely used that it was not thought worth while to include them. COMPLEX type gets only a passing mention.

## Acknowledgments

Although I should find it virtually impossible to manage without the support of my wife, Yvonne, she seems to have done very well without mine during the period of this book's preparation, for which I am extremely grateful. My daughter, Karen, has been of great help in the debugging of the text and many of the algorithms in it. Naturally, if any errors remain the fault is mine. I shall be very glad to hear of them, care of the publisher.

Arthur Radford

# 1

# Introduction

Computers have been with us now since the mid-1940s, and it would probably not be overstating the case to say that they have brought about a revolution in our way of life, though this may not be immediately apparent to the man in the street. To take two instances: without the computer the world's banking institutions would be unable to cope with the volume of business they have and, in all probability, man would still be trying to figure out some means of getting to the moon – and back – safely.

Early computers were bulky and expensive, needing specially air-conditioned environments; by contrast, some 30 years later, there is available a large range of microcomputers, some costing less than a single week's salary for an average working man, small enough to be carried and able to be connected to a domestic power supply in an ordinary living room. Amazingly, this modern system is, in many respects, equal to or better than its bulky ancestor.

Ever since man first started to count and began to appreciate the power and use of numbers, he has sought ways of increasing the speed with which he could handle them. The human brain is a marvellous machine, but it is – except very occasionally when a numeric prodigy is born – pitifully slow at performing arithmetic processes, by comparison with a modern computer. On the other hand, the rate at which the brain can store and retrieve information is generally much faster than that of the machine, and its memory capacity is also enormous.

Man has always tried to augment his natural calculating ability by one means or another. At first he must have counted on his fingers, which may explain why our most commonly used number system is based on the number 10. Later, primitive calculating devices appeared, such as the abacus whose efficiency may be judged from the fact that, even today, it is still used all over the world. The slide rule and desk calculating machines, the punched card, transistor and now the 'microchip' all lead inexorably to the modern computer. This does not mean that the idea of a machine capable of automatically performing a sequence of arithmetic and logical operations is particularly new: Charles Babbage (1792–1871) designed and built what might be described as the first computer, in the sense that we understand the term today, though it was mechanical in nature rather than electronic. His 'analytical engine' embodied in its design many of the principles of the modern computer, but its construction – begun in 1833 – was never completed because it was not then possible to engineer the parts with the required tolerances. His great friend and supporter was Ada, Lady Lovelace, sometimes referred to as the first programmer. As recently as 1980, she has been honoured by the appearance of a new computer language commissioned by the US Department of Defense and called, simply, ADA.

## The modern computer

Towards the end of the Second World War the first true electronic computers appeared, and they were very different from those used today. Rarely has an industry developed in such a brief period or have new techniques been perfected so rapidly as has been the case with the computer. The first machine, ENIAC (electronic numerical integrator and calculator), represented a tremendous step forward, but was little more than a clumsy toy by comparison with the larger machines of today, whose calculating speeds are measured in millions of instructions per second (mips).

A very important early development was the introduction of the *stored program* concept – the list of instructions that tells the computer what operations it is to perform and the order in which it shall perform them (the *program*) are *read* from punched cards, punched paper tape or, with a modern computer, directly from a typewriter-like *terminal keyboard* and held in the machine's *memory*, or *store*. There is no need for the computer to be given its instructions one at a time by the human operator, or some electromechanical device; all the instructions are in the machine from the start and can be selected in the right order quite automatically at electronic speeds. Particular groups of instructions can be repeated as many times as necessary; the next instruction to be obeyed can be decided at the time the program is executed depending on the results of previous calculations performed by the program – we have, in fact, a very flexible system capable of undertaking a great deal of boring and repetitive calculation, leaving the human user to concentrate on the more creative and 'people-oriented' aspects of his job.

One example of such repetition occurs in the calculation of weekly wages for a firm employing a large number of staff. A computer can do this very well, since the arithmetic is very straightforward and the process of determining net pay from gross pay taking the various deductions for income tax, social security, etc. is well defined. But if it is necessary to load the computer with the program after each wage slip has been printed, the whole thing becomes impractical. If the program is stored in the machine's memory, however, the calculations can be repeated as many times as is necessary, using the same sequence of instructions over and over again, entering new data for each employee in turn.

The early 1950s saw the commercial introduction of the stored-program computer – the so-called 'first-generation' machines, which were produced for some eight or nine years before giving way to the faster and more economical 'second generation' of machines. These used transistor circuitry, a great advance which led on through miniaturisation into integrated circuits and the 'third generation' of computers. Now, large-scale integration is widely used: the microchip is with us, causing equipment prices to plummet and computing speeds to soar. And, of course, there is great interest in personal computers for home entertainment and small business applications.

Early computers were quite difficult to program, and it was necessary to engage very skilled people to do the job, often with advanced mathematical qualifications. This tended to limit the applications to which these machines were turned, though a great deal of very important work was completed, and many new techniques were discovered during this period. Sadly, computing has never shaken off the mystique it gathered in those early days, and most people still seem to think, wrongly, that you have to be a mathematician to be a computer programmer.

The main difficulty was then – as it is today with some microsystems – the need to write programs in what is known as *machine language*, or *machine code*. This requires that the programmer has an intimate and detailed knowledge of the workings of the machine, and that he gives explicit instructions to the computer for every operation to be performed – even the most fundamental. It is necessary, for example, to state exactly where, in its memory, the machine will store the data it is to use and where the result of each intermediate calculation is to be held; he must know precisely the content of each of the machine's registers, and a host of other fiddling details. Worse, it may be necessary to express these instructions in a numerical code, and these coded values would quite probably be in some number system other than the decimal system, based on 10, with which we are most familiar. At worst, we might be obliged to use the binary system, based on 2, in which the number 123, for instance, is written as 1111011. More likely, using a modern microcomputer, if it were necessary to use machine code, instructions would be expressed in hexadecimal, or base 16, notation. The hexadecimal representation of 123 is 7B – yes, we use letters as well as digits, because there are not enough different digits!

The form of machine language differs from machine to machine, since it is very closely tied to the design of the computer. This usually means that programs written in the machine language of one computer cannot be executed on any machine other than one of exactly the same type. It follows that a great deal of work must be duplicated, and the problem is particularly serious when a new computer of a different type is installed. A further implication is that if a person has learnt to program one computer in its machine language, he is likely to have to spend a lot of time relearning when a new computer replaces it. Another disadvantage of machine language programming is that it is a specialist business – the originator of a problem is unlikely to have the necessary skill to be able to express its solution in the form of a machine-language program. This can be a great disadvantage, for the programmer is equally likely to be ignorant of the field to which the problem applies. So we have a communication barrier, and the problem is worsened if the program has to be changed frequently, or there is a rapid turnover in programming staff, as often happens.

The solution to this problem was to make programming languages more easily learnt, and to make them portable – relatively easy to transfer from one computer to others of different types. It was realised that there was a need to raise the 'level' of the language above that of the basic machine code, away from the machine and towards the problem, so that it became more like that used by mathematicians, or businessmen. So it was that the *high-level languages* began to appear.

The first of these were called *autocodes*, and they had instructions which were very similar in appearance to simple algebraic formulae. The expression $b^2 - 4ac$ might have been encoded as follows:

```
X = 4 * A
X = X * C
Y = B * B
X = Y — X
```

Here, an asterisk (*) has been used to indicate the operation of multiplication. The '=' sign does not have its normal mathematical meaning, but has to be interpreted as 'is assigned the value of'. Note how it is possible to represent only very simple operations, the given expression needing four autocode instructions. However, it would need at least twice that number of machine code instructions, which means we have a significant saving in time and a more comprehensible program.

The computer, of course, is unchanged. Each machine continued to recognise only its own machine language. Somehow, the autocode instructions had to be translated into machine language before they could be executed. This is a fairly simple procedure that can be specified exactly, and can be written, in machine code, as a computer program. Once this has been done, the computer itself can read the autocode instructions, translate them into the corresponding machine-language instructions, and store them away in its memory. When all the instructions have been dealt with, it can then start to execute the program it has stored – all quite automatically.

The writing of the translator program was – and is – a skilled process, needing an extensive knowledge of the computer. But it only has to be written once, after which the bulk of the work can be done using the autocode. The problem of machine dependence remains, however, because autocodes were generally designed with a particular machine, or group of machines, in mind, and programs written for one family of machines were likely to be unusable with a different family unless they were extensively modified. They were, however, considerably more readable, and the task of rewriting thus became rather less of a chore. Nevertheless, something rather more machine independent and more oriented towards the needs of the user was needed. Thus FORTRAN was born.

## FORTRAN

The arrival of FORTRAN heralded a new era in computer programming, for it enabled programs to be expressed in a form very similar to that used in everyday mathematical notation. It was developed in the USA by the well-known computer manufacturer, IBM, and was quickly adopted by the manufacturers of other equipment as a general-purpose computer language, largely independent of any particular machine, but capable of being translated into efficient machine code. FORTRAN is an acronym for FORmula TRANslator, and it has become one of the most widely adopted computer languages for serious scientific and engineering applications. In 1966, the language was standardised by the American National Standards Institute(ANSI), and 11 years later a new standard, FORTRAN 77, was published. This version is now being implemented by many computer manufacturers for their equipment, and it is this language with which this book is primarily concerned. Complete coverage is not possible in a book of this nature: the language is completely defined as an American National Standard in the document 'ANSI X3.9–1978: Programming Language FORTRAN'. Copies are available from the American National Standards Institute, 1430 Broadway, New York, NY 10018, USA.

The following oversimplified example should give an idea of the appearance of a FORTRAN program. Suppose that a large number of measurements have been taken of lengths, all expressed in feet, and it is required to convert them into kilometres. We can express this as a formula relating the distance in kilometres, DIST, to the number of feet, FEET, thus:

```
DIST = FEET / 3280.84
```

using the symbol '/' to denote division, and where 3280.84 is the number of feet in a kilometre. We can use the formula as it stands – it is an instruction (more properly, a *statement*) in the FORTRAN language. Unfortunately, it only shows the way in which a single length may be converted, and it would not, in practice, be economical to use a commercial computer system for such a small problem. So let us be a little more realistic and assume that there are 5000 measurements to be converted.

The basic process for a computer program would be to read a length value (in feet) into computer memory, perform the conversion calculation, print out the result, and repeat the set of operations another 4999 times. The following is a FORTRAN 77 program which could be used to achieve this.

```
      PROGRAM CONVRT
      DO 10, N = 1, 5000
      READ *, FEET
      DIST = FEET / 3280.84
  10  PRINT *, FEET, DIST
      END
```

Let us take it a line at a time.

```
      PROGRAM CONVRT
```

This simply gives the program as a whole a name, by which you can refer to it, if you wish to do so. There is no obligation to use a PROGRAM statement, but if you do it has to be the first in the program.

```
      DO 10, N = 1, 5000
```

DO (i.e. obey, or execute) the statements which follow as far as, and including, the one labelled 10, 5000 times. This is achieved by setting the variable N to 1 initially, increasing this value by 1 each time the group of three statements that follow is executed, and terminating the repetition when the count reaches 5000

```
      READ *, FEET
```

Read a number from the standard input device and call it FEET.

```
DIST = FEET / 3280.84
```

Divide the value called FEET by 3280.84 and call the result DIST. This is the central conversion process.

```
10 PRINT *, FEET, DIST
```

This statement has the label 10 at the left. The values of FEET and DIST are printed (or displayed in some other fashion) on the standard output device. Then N is increased by 1, and we go back to the READ if N is less than 5000.

```
END
```

This is self-explanatory; the program terminates here.

We shall deal in detail with each of these statement types, and a number of others, in the body of this book.

You will notice that the program uses English and mathematical notation and, with a little practice, is quite easy to read and understand, unlike machine code. The user of FORTRAN needs to know very little about the computer that will execute the instructions of his program, though it may help in particular, specialised, applications if he does know something of his machine's 'architecture', so that he can 'tune' his program to work at maximum efficiency. Inevitably, however, such programs tend to be less portable than those that are written with no particular computer in mind.

Again, the computer will only be able to recognise its own machine code, and so the FORTRAN program will have to be translated into that language. This is a much more formidable task than the translation of an autocode program, but it is a task that a computer can be programmed to perform quickly and efficiently. At this level, the translation process is called *compilation* (because machine code instructions – or something very closely resembling them – are *compiled* into a program), and the program that accomplishes this is usually known as a *compiler*.

## The compilation process

A compiler is a *program* and is usually supplied with the computer system. If the computer is a small one, the compiler may be supplied on a reel of paper tape, or on a cassette tape such as you would use on your cassette recorder. Compilers for microcomputers are often permanently held in ROM (read-only memory) 'chips' and are plugged into special memory sockets in the computer when needed. A FORTRAN 77 compiler is rather a large program, however, and is unlikely to be available in this form. There are many other recording media that are used: $\frac{1}{2}$-inch magnetic tape, magnetic discs in a variety of sizes, and punched cards – all these are very popular and likely to be used to hold the compilers needed by a computer. The important point is for it to be possible to read the compiler from whatever medium it is recorded on into the main memory of the computer, where it will be held in the form of machine-language instructions. It is then activated, and your program, originally written in FORTRAN but now probably punched on cards or paper tape, is read in under the control of the compiler and translated into machine language. Your program is called the *source code*, and the output from the compiler is the *object code*. This object code may be stored in the machine's main memory, ready for immediate execution, or it may be output to one of the auxiliary 'backing storage' devices which most modern computers have. From here it can be loaded back into memory at any time and executed.

A very important feature of the compilation process is the production of *diagnostic messages* by the compiler. As each FORTRAN statement is encountered by the compiler it is scanned carefully and checked for language errors. FORTRAN has its grammatical rules, just like any other language, and unless the rules are observed by the person writing the program the compiler will be unable to determine what the programmer intends and hence will not be able to generate the required machine code. Such errors are called *syntax errors*, and the checking process ensures that ambiguous or meaningless instructions are detected. It is a fact of life, which has to be accepted by programmers very early in their careers, that most programs will contain syntax errors when first compiled: do not let this discourage you. Certainly, try to avoid them as far as possible by becoming very familiar with the language through practice; even so, you will make minor errors, or miscopying will occur in typing or keypunching your program. These should be picked up on the first compilation or so. Try not to regard such things as commas or quotation marks as insignificant –

they are not. The meaning may be apparent to a human reader, but compilers are much more pedantic than people. Pay attention to detail when writing your programs, and do it with care. Do not, for instance – as many beginners are prone to do – let your pencil rest on the paper if you do not want a mark; the chances are it will leave a dot, and this may well be typed as if it were part of your program, producing a syntax error.

It will often happen that, even if the syntax is correct, there is a fault in the *logic*, or design, of your program. This cannot be detected by the compiler and will be revealed during program execution – at *runtime* – when unexpected results are obtained. Such runtime errors can be very difficult to track down, and we shall have more to say about this aspect later.

It is not enough to know that there is a syntax error in one's program, and the better compilers will do all in their power to pinpoint the source of the error. Smaller systems may do this by printing a simple *error code*, such as

    113: UL

meaning that an undefined label was noticed on line 113. More sophisticated systems will print a detailed description of the error, with an indication of its probable cause. If the syntax is not quite right, but the meaning can be inferred, a lot of compilers are able to take limited remedial action, issue a warning message and carry on as if nothing had happened. But when the error cannot be corrected – a so-called *fatal* error condition – compilation of machine language will usually cease, though the error scan will continue. In this way, even though the program is not compiled and so cannot be executed, it is at least examined thoroughly for possible syntax faults.

## System control

How is it, you may have wondered, that the computer is able to activate the compiler just at the moment it is needed? And how are the other seemingly completely automatic operations performed, such as reading in your program, ensuring that your results do not get jumbled up with someone else's, abandoning your compilation if it goes catastrophically wrong, and transferring attention to the next job? The reason is that many computers will have in their memory a set of programs collectively known as the *operating system*, which has a supervisory function and controls the overall operation of the machine, ensuring that the various processes that have to be performed are nicely synchronised. Different computer manufacturers tend to have different names for the operating system – supervisor, master control program, executive – but the effect is the same. Every aspect of the processing of programs and the operation of the machine's peripheral devices (such as card readers, magnetic storage devices, printers, etc.) comes under the control of the operating system. It also controls multiprogramming, a system whereby several different programs appear to execute simultaneously, ensuring that the facilities of the computer are used in an optimal manner and keeping wastage of resources, such as memory space, to a minimum. This is important, since computers are expensive to install and operate and must be kept fully employed if their use is to be economically justified. This is the case with the larger commercial systems, at any rate. The advent of the microcomputer makes this not quite so important for smaller systems.

The world of the computer is, unfortunately, riddled with acronyms and jargon terms. These you will rapidly become familiar with if you work in a data processing department. Two of the most common terms – now often used outside the computing environment – are *hardware* and *software*. Hardware is easy enough to define: the hard parts of the computer, the bits you can touch, constitute its hardware. Software consists of the programs that the computer system needs to fulfill its day-to-day commitments. The operating system is a collection of programs and constitutes a major item of software. Associated with it are all manner of auxiliary programs: compilers, sorting routines, copying programs – everyday stuff needed to keep the system running. These too are items of software. The quality of the software supplied with a computer can make or mar the efficiency of the system as a whole.

Since FORTRAN programs have first to be compiled into machine language, they take longer to process than the equivalent programs written in a form closer to machine language. (Machine-language programs are not often written for commercial and scientific applications these days, but there are languages known as *assembly languages* that are very closely related to it. They are, however, much easier to learn and to use.) Longer processing time means that more machine time is needed, which in turn implies a higher cost per program. This is offset by the fact that programs are written very much more quickly in FORTRAN, or any other high-level language, than they would be in assembly language and they are usually more easily checked out and maintained if anything goes wrong.

The compiler itself is also very important. If it works slowly, the cost of using it is increased, but it is likely to produce a more efficient object code. A faster compiler may not optimise the code produced to the same extent, and the resulting object code may run more slowly or take up more memory space. Different circumstances call for different attacks on the problem, but a long program that is to be used frequently will usually need to be as fast in operation as one can reasonably make it. The economy may not be so important when a job is to be performed only once or twice. Many machines have two FORTRAN compilers, one which optimises its compiled code and one which does not. These are sometimes combined, and the programmer can specify by means of an instruction at the head of his program whether he wants the code optimised. During the checkout phase of developing his program, he will normally specify no optimisation. When the program is working correctly, he may well recompile it with the optimisation option set. Thus all requirements can be met with a single compiler.

## Programming

The process of writing a program is quite straightforward. The trouble is, especially with newcomers to programming, that there is an enormous temptation to get in there and write some code, submit it to the computer and see if it has worked. Unfortunately, if this attitude is taken, it will usually be found that it has not worked, and much toil will be needed to persuade it to do so.

It is essential that the problem under consideration for computer solution be subjected to very careful and detailed analysis. The computer will only do those operations that it is instructed to perform, so the instructions of your program must specify *exactly* what is to be done – no more, and certainly no less. All possibilities must be allowed for, although it is very easy not to realise what all the possibilities are. For example, if a program does not contain an instruction to STOP, it will continue working until it is stopped by the intervention of the operator, or the operating system, and is quite likely, as a result, to produce some unexpected answers.

Before any problem can be solved using a computer, the person writing the program must be very familiar with both the problem and the method to be used in solving it (often called the *algorithm*). The solution must be expressed as a sequence of simple steps that the machine can execute one after the other until the solution is achieved. This will often mean the presentation of a series of algebraic formulae to the machine, together with an indication of the criteria needed for it to take certain logical decisions at key points of the calculation. Frequently required functions will be available in a 'program library', so that it is not necessary to write routines for the calculation of square roots or commonly used trigonometrical functions, etc.

It is thus necessary to concentrate on the analysis of the problem and the development of a good algorithm. Once this has been done, assuming a certain familiarity with the computer language to be used – in this case FORTRAN 77 – the actual writing of the program is almost a mechanical process. In the next chapter, we shall consider the development of the algorithm in more detail.

# 2

# Program design

In Chapter 1 we saw that a computer will only respond to simple instructions. This implies that the solution to a problem, if it is to be undertaken by a computer, will have to be expressed as a sequence of elementary steps. We now have to emphasise a very important point: computers do not solve problems, in general. The problem is solved by the analyst or programmer. Of course, the calculation involved may well be so complex or lengthy that he would not have the time to follow it through and obtain the answers, but once the method of solution is established, the problem is solved. We have to express the algorithm in a way that the computer can 'understand' leaving it to grind away at high speed until the results appear. The task of the computer is to relieve the tedium of repetitive numerical calculation.

Before we can write a FORTRAN program, then, we must be quite sure that we have understood the problem to be solved. This is not always easy; people are not very good at explaining exactly what it is they want, and problems are often couched in extremely woolly terms. It is essential to keep pestering the client until both parties are convinced that the problem statement is sufficiently precise that it is completely understood by all concerned.

Next, we have to establish in detail the sequence of operations to be performed in order to produce the required results. This is the program design phase, in which the *logic* of the program is worked out. Unless the logic is correct, there is no hope of producing a correctly working program, and it is here that the craft of the programmer lies. Given a good, clear design, the program almost writes itself. Without it, something close to chaos can result, but it may be some time before we realise this, and a lot of time and money can have been poured into the project by then.

## Flowcharts

Most people will have used a shopping list at some time. In many ways such a list is rather like a program: first call at the butcher, then at the grocer's, then the hardware shop, check the petrol when passing the garage, and so on. The list helps to plan a shopping trip by specifying the sequence of events – the trip's logic. Drawing up the shopping list is a process of program design, for a human computer.

In designing a computer algorithm, there are a number of ways in which we can represent it. Quite often a narrative form, similar to the shopping list, is suitable. Indeed, such forms are becoming quite popular and are often referred to as *design code*, or *pseudocode*. Later, we shall give examples of these. For the moment, let us consider an alternative and very popular way of specifying an algorithm – the graphical method known as the *flowchart*. The events within the process are shown as boxes, the shape of the box indicates the type of event, and the order in which these events are to occur is specified by joining the boxes together with lines. Arrowheads are placed on the lines, where necessary, to make the direction of flow quite clear.

All this is best illustrated by showing an example of a flowchart. Let us use the shopping trip already mentioned for our example. Suppose that we leave home by car, drive to the shops, then call at the butcher, the grocer and the hardware store, in that order. Having done this, we check the petrol in the car. If the level is low, then we should call in at the garage to fill up the tank. Finally, we drive back home. Fig. 2.1 is a flowchart for this outing. Each of the boxes indicates a task to be performed, and the lines indicate the order in which the tasks are to be executed. Note that the start point, the finish point and the point at which a decision is made are all clearly marked by distinctively shaped boxes.

Flowcharts may be used to clarify complicated decision processes. An example is given in Fig. 2.2, which shows the process of sorting letters. This is a simple operation, but it involves a

**Fig. 2.1**

multiway decision when the sorter, with a letter in his hand, has to decide which of the pigeonholes in front of him has to receive it. If you look carefully at the chart, in which the decision has been reduced to a choice of three possibilities, you will see that the logic forms a loop which stops only when there is no more mail to be sorted. This flowchart contains a possible 'bug' (error): if a letter turns up which is addressed to some place other than London, Cardiff or Belfast, we shall not know what to do, since the chart does not give any instructions for this situation. One way out of this problem would be to introduce another branch marked 'OTHER' and include instructions as to what to do in such a case. Alternatively, a disclaimer could be used, such as 'Users of this chart must validate letters before starting to ensure that only those addressed to London, Cardiff or Belfast are processed'.

Loops such as this are commonly encountered. The computer's ability to perform such repetitions automatically is one of its most powerful features, and we shall meet it frequently. The arrowheads on the flowlines indicate the order in which the boxes are to be 'visited'. They are not always given, the convention being that normal flow is from the top towards the bottom of the chart, and from the left towards the right-hand side. Where the flow is not in accordance with the convention, *or at any point where there might be ambiguity*, arrowheads should be added to the flowlines.

These two examples probably seem to have little relevance to the problem of making use of a computer. But the principle of reducing a complex sequence of events and decisions into an ordered grouping using a device such as a flowchart to keep track of the logic is one of general application, and the importance of spending time on the design of a program before coding starts cannot be overemphasised. As a programmer becomes more experienced, he may become less dependent on flowcharts for simpler problems, and this may be all right for a 'one-off' job that has to be got working quickly and may never be used again. For a production program – one which may be used regularly for years – it is essential that it be documented carefully, so that any changes that may be needed (for instance, changes in Social Security deductions, in a payroll application) can be quickly incorporated. The flowchart or design code will form a very important part of any such program documentation, since the way in which the program works is usually

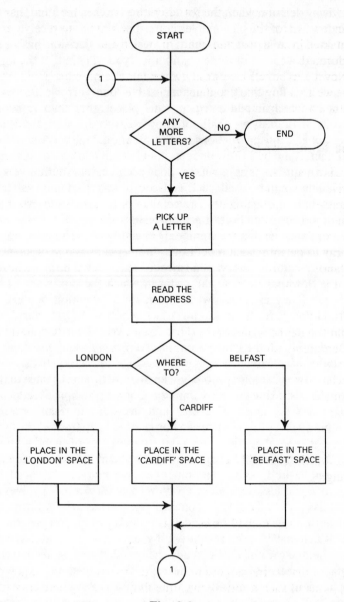

**Fig. 2.2**

shown much more clearly in this description of the algorithm than it is in the statements of the program itself; the mass of detail contained in most programs tends to mask the basic processes being performed.

Now let us have a look at some more problems – this time of the type we are more likely to meet using FORTRAN 77. The first is a mathematical example.

## The Fibonacci series

This is a sequence of numbers in which each number of the series is derived from the values of the two numbers that immediately precede it in the sequence. The value of each term is given by the sum of the two numbers that precede it in the series. It follows that once we have defined the values of the first two terms in the series we can calculate the values of as many other terms as we wish. For instance, suppose that the first two terms each have the value 1. That is to say, the series starts off looking like this:

   1   1   . . .

What will be the values of the third, fourth, and subsequent terms?

Bearing in mind the way in which the series is defined, namely that each term must be equal in value to the sum of the two preceding terms, the third term must be equal in value to the second term added to the first term. That is to say, $1 + 1 = 2$. We now have:

   1   1   2   . . .

The fourth term will be the sum of the third and second terms, giving:

   1   1   2   3   . . .

and so on. The first 10 terms will be:

   1   1   2   3   5   8   13   21   34   55   . . . .

Suppose that a program has to be written to compute the values of the terms of such a series, given the first two terms, and that 100 terms are required altogether. The detailed preparation of the program is beyond us at the moment, but that is not where we should start, anyway. We shall draw up a flowchart representing the algorithm for the process. Where *do* we start? The first two terms may both have the value 1, but this is not necessarily so, and we should allow for their being changed by the user of the program; perhaps we should arrange that the values of these terms be read in at the beginning of the program.

We can make a list showing the sequence of events that must occur:

1 Read in the values of the first and second terms and print them.
2 Add these together to form the third term and print this.
3 Add the second and third terms to form the fourth term and print it.
4 Add the third and fourth terms to form the fifth term and print it.
5 Add the fourth and fifth terms . . . ' etc.

It is already beginning to get a little bit tedious. Rather than write a new section of program for the calculation of each successive term, we can set up a loop. The flowchart in Fig. 2.3 shows one way in which this problem might be approached, and it was developed from the following piece of design code:

1 Read the first two values.
2 Set a count = 3.
3 While the count does not exceed 100:
   (a) Calculate the value of the next term.
   (b) Add 1 to the count:
4 Print the complete set of 100 values.
5 End.

In the flowchart, each term of the series is denoted by the letter *a* to which a *subscript* had been attached. Thus, $a_1$ is the first term, $a_2$ is the second, $a_{29}$ the twenty-ninth, and so on. Each term will, of course, have a numerical value, but it is convenient to use a symbol such as *a* to define a general solution.

If you look at Fig. 2.3, after the START box at the head of the chart, you will see that the first action is the reading of the values for the first two terms. In the next box, the symbol *i* is introduced. This is the count mentioned in the design code; the value of *i* is the subscript of the next term to be computed. So when *i* is greater than 100, we shall have calculated as many terms as we need. Symbols such as *a* and *i*, which are used to name values that can vary during the execution of the program, are called *variables*. At this stage, since we want to calculate the value of the third term next, the variable *i* is given the value 3.

The next box is a test to determine whether or not the value of the 100th term has been calculated; if it has, the value of *i* will exceed 100. The first time through, since we set the value of *i* to 3, this test will fail and the NO exit will be taken.

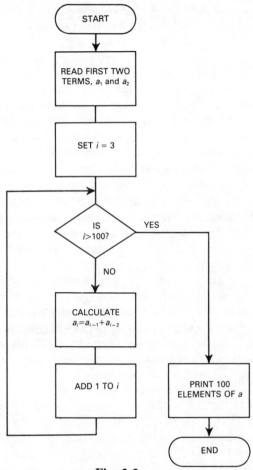

START

READ FIRST TWO TERMS, $a_1$ and $a_2$

SET $i = 3$

IS $i > 100$?

YES

NO

CALCULATE $a_i = a_{i-1} + a_{i-2}$

ADD 1 TO $i$

PRINT 100 ELEMENTS OF $a$

END

**Fig. 2.3**

The next box specifies that a formula is to be used:

$$a_i = a_{i-1} + a_{i-2}$$

and, since $i$ has the value 3, this first time through, we can interpret the formula as meaning

$$a_3 = a_2 + a_1.$$

This, of course, defines the value of the third term of our Fibonacci series – the sum of the two immediately preceding terms.

The next action is to increase the value of $i$ by 1 and loop back to the test, which will again fail. We shall calculate

$$a_4 = a_3 + a_2$$

because $i$ now has the value 4.

The process continues until the value of $i$ is eventually increased from 100 to 101. This time the test will succeed, the YES exit will be taken from the test and we can proceed to print the 100 elements of $a$, which now represent the Fibonacci series. The task is done and the chart terminates in the box marked END.

The observant reader will have noticed that his algorithm does not correspond exactly to the original list of steps, in that we have computed all the values before printing any of them. This was to avoid the special case of terms 1 and 2 being printed separately. Fig. 2.4 is another flowchart for the production of the same series, but is more economical because it does not require the whole series to be stored before output is initiated. At each stage, only the two terms needed for the calculation of the next term are retained, and those not needed are discarded after the output. Notice that we have to print inside the loop in this case and that there is a special process for terms 1 and 2. A careful study of this example should be quite rewarding. The corresponding FORTRAN 77 program is quite simple and is given below.

```
      PROGRAM FIB
      READ *, A1, A2
      PRINT *, A1, A2
      DO 10, I = 3, 100
         A3 = A1 + A2
         PRINT *, A3
         A1 = A2
   10    A2 = A3
      END
```

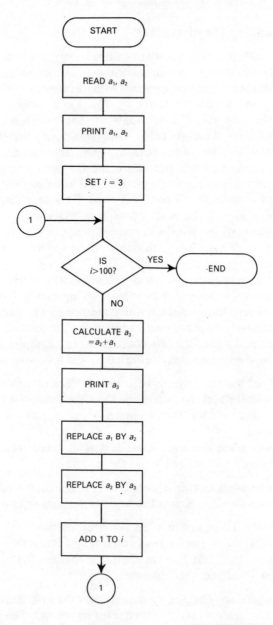

**Fig. 2.4**

## Counting the characters

The authenticity of a piece of writing – story, poem or letter – can be determined by comparing the frequency with which common words appear in the text being studied with frequencies determined from a study of similar material by the same author about whose authenticity there is no doubt. If the two texts show similar frequencies of use, there is a strong probability that they have been written by the same person. This description is very much simplified, but sets the scene for the next example, which is concerned with reading a piece of text and determining how many times a particular *character* is used. This simplifies the problem somewhat, but the basic principle is exactly the same if we are counting words. We shall need to know when we get to the end of the text; I shall assume that this can be tested after an attempt to read.

One very successful and recommended method of program design is that known as the 'top-down' approach. One starts with a broad description of the solution method and proceeds in stages by successively breaking each complicated process down into several more easily handled procedures. In our example, a suitable first attempt might be that illustrated by the following design code:

1 Read the character to be counted. Perform any initialisation.
2 Read the text characters one at a time, comparing each with the target character. When a match is found, add one to a character count.
3 Stop when the end of the text is detected, after printing the character and the value of the count.

This is rather lacking in detail, but gives us a starting point. Let us expand step 2, which is the heart of the algorithm.

2 While the end of text has not been reached:
   (a) If the character read is the target character
       then add 1 to the character count.
   (b) Read the next character.

Here, we are obviously assuming that the first character has been read, because we start with a test for end of text. This will have to be part of the initialisation in step 1. We shall also need to set the character count to 0 when we initialise, because to start with we have not read any instances of the target character. So step 1 might finish up looking like this:

1 (a) Read the target character (i.e. the one which is to be counted).
   (b) Set the character count to 0.
   (c) Read the next character.

Finally, we can expand step 3:

3 (a) Print the target character.
   (b) Print the character count.
   (c) End.

Bringing the three expanded steps together, we have this:

1 (a) Read the target character.
   (b) Set the character count to 0.
   (c) Read the next text character.
2 While the end of text has not been reached:
   (a) If the character read is the target character
       then add 1 to the character count.
   (b) Read the next text character.
3 (a) Print the target character.
   (b) Print the character count.
   (c) End.

This is expressed as a flowchart in Fig. 2.5. The equivalent FORTRAN 77 program is not given here, since character manipulation raises problems that are better dealt with later.

## A payroll calculation

As the final example in this chapter, consider the case of a program designed to perform wage calculations. In practice, this is quite a complicated problem, for there are many factors to be taken into account; income tax at various rates, social security deductions, bonus payments, savings deductions, and so on, all increase the complexity of the logic. Basically, however, the problem is a straightforward one: we have to multiply the number of hours worked by the employee by the hourly rate of pay and make any

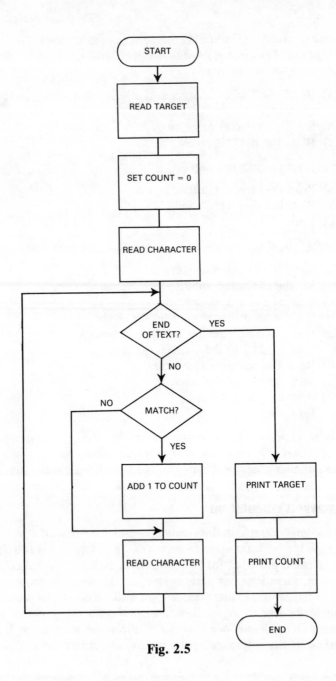

**Fig. 2.5**

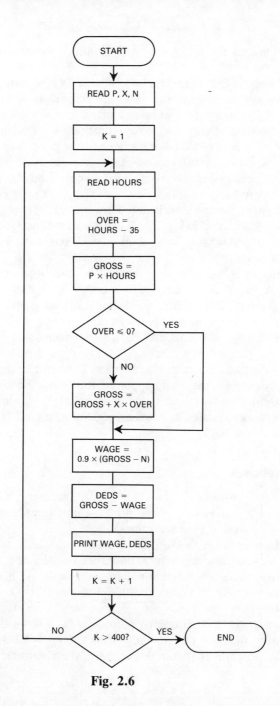

**Fig. 2.6**

deductions for taxes, etc. and additions for overtime working, etc.

Suppose that a firm employs 400 weekly paid men, each working a 35-hour week, anything above this being classed as overtime. The rate of pay is P pence per hour, and to this is added x pence per hour of overtime worked. (So the overtime rate is P + x pence per hour.) Social Security deductions amount to N pence per week. Other deductions amount to one-tenth of what remains after Social Security has been taken out. It would be a good idea at this point if you were to try to draw a flowchart showing the way in which each employee's wage is calculated each week. Then compare your version with that in Fig. 2.6; it will not be identical, but be sure you understand what is being done in each box as well as the overall procedure.

HOURS is the total time worked by each employee during the week; WAGE is the final payment after all deductions have been made. DEDS is the sum of the deductions, and OVER is the number of hours of overtime worked by the employee. GROSS is the wage before any deductions have been made. Notice that a check is made to see whether OVER is negative; why do you think this is? OVER will be negative if an employee happens to work less than the normal 35-hour week; see what happens in this case if the test is *not* made.

Before you continue to the next chapter, try some or all of the following exercises in flowcharting. Solutions will be found at the end of the book.

## Exercises

1 Add together the first 50 natural numbers (i.e. $1 + 2 + 3 + 4 \ldots$ ) and print the final sum. Note that you are *not* asked to read the values!

2 Convert a length expressed in inches into yards, feet and inches.

3 A chemical manufacturer publishes a catalogue in which each of his products is listed in dollars per pound. He has uncovered a new market in France, but his customers there require to know the prices in francs per kilogramme. Given that he currently produces 250 different products, what will be the conversion procedure? (1 dollar = 6.56 francs; 1 kg = 2.2 lb).

4 A program is required to classify the results of examinations

taken by a large group of candidates. There are to be four classes: 80% or more (distinction), 60–79% (credit), 40–59% (pass) and less than 40% (fail).

It is required to count the number of results in each group. Assume that there were 10 000 candidates. The program should print four lines: the number of distinctions, then the number of credits, next the number of passes and, finally, the number of failures. Draw a flowchart for this program.

5 A transport company needs to analyse the fuel consumption of its vehicle fleet. For each vehicle, the number of miles driven and the amount of fuel consumed during a test period are known. Suppose that the fleet has N vehicles. Design the algorithm to tabulate the average fuel consumption of each vehicle given, the vehicle number and the values mentioned above.

6 In a certain year, the income tax paid by a married man without children was calculated as follows: Two-ninths of his total income, plus a further sum of £240.00, was free of tax. The remainder, called the *taxable income*, was charged in accordance with the following rules.

The first £50.00 was taxed at 11p in the £ (there are 100p per £); the next £150.00 was taxed at 34p in the pound; and on any further taxable income the rate was 43p in the pound.

Design an algorithm for the computation of the tax payable by each of a group of 500 employees.

# 3

# Dealing with numbers

It is time we got down to business; before long you will be writing programs in FORTRAN, but first we shall have to look at some of the basic ideas of the language. You will possibly find some of the rules rather strange at first, unduly restrictive and sometimes unreasonable. But all languages have to have rules and FORTRAN is no exception; please ensure that the rules given in this chapter and throughout the rest of the book are carefully observed in every program you write.

Did you understand the implications of the previous paragraph. It doesn't really matter whether you answer 'yes' or 'no' – either response indicates that you have understood the question. But if you were a computer the chances are that you would not have been able to understand, since the sentence contains a syntax error: it has no question mark at the end. Your imagination and previous experience will have enabled you to supply the missing piece of syntactic information, but a computer would not normally have been able to do so. As a result, it would either have produced a diagnostic message or thought it understood, gone on blindly and produced a nonsense answer. You really *have* to appreciate that if a computer program is presented with meaningless data it will produce meaningless results.

Computers are not infallible: both the program and the data supplied to it must be free of errors before the answers can be considered reliable. All that computers do is to obey instructions – in this respect they are very reliable and the hardware rarely goes wrong – and the instructions must be presented to them in a very precisely defined form. Your computer will not guess; if an instruction is nonsense, the machine will probably stop and rely on human intervention to put things right. So why use such unintelligent devices? The answer lies in the precision with which they follow orders and the speed with which they can carry out logical processes such as arithmetic; this makes them far superior to the human brain for performing routine calculating tasks in which speed and accuracy are of primary importance. Accuracy when programming is essential, not only when designing the algorithm but also when writing down the instructions that will implement it. You will be using a computer language – FORTRAN – but you will need to be far more careful to obey all the rules than would be the case if you were learning a natural language such as French or Italian. Luckily, there are not all that many rules to learn and there is usually a reference book nearby.

## Constants

Here is a very simple FORTRAN program.

```
PROGRAM CIRCUM
PARAMETER (PI = 3.14159)
READ *, RADIUS
CIRC = 2 * PI * RADIUS
PRINT *, 'RADIUS:',RADIUS,'CIRCUMFERENCE:',CIRC
END
```

Its purpose is to calculate and print the circumference of a circle, given the radius. The simple formula connecting radius and circumference is circumference $= 2\pi \times$ radius, where $\pi$ is the Greek letter 'pi', which is frequently used by mathematicians, engineers and scientists to represent the ratio of the circumference of a circle to its diameter: its value is unchanging at about 3.14159. This value is called a *constant*; it does not change, regardless of the circumstances. 3.14159 always has the value 3.14159.

Any number is a constant. The program contains another example, the number 2; 2 is always 2, so it is also a constant. Another example is 747. Obviously, constants may be either whole numbers or numbers with a fraction part. 747 is a whole number constant, 1.8 is a constant with a fraction part.

There is an important difference between these two types of

constant: 1.8 contains a decimal point, whereas 747 does not. When we do arithmetic in everyday life, we tend to take decimal points very much for granted. It does not normally matter whether we express a constant as 20 or as 20.0, for if the decimal point is omitted from a whole number, we still understand what is intended, and in practice both representations mean the same thing. To the FORTRAN compiler, however, there is a very important difference between 20 and 20.0, though both are constants. The form *without* the decimal point is treated internally in a rather different way from the form *with* a point, and it is necessary to take a little care in deciding which representation to use when writing your programs. In what follows, constants which do *not* contain a decimal point will be referred to as INTEGER constants, while those which *do* have a decimal point will be called REAL constants. You may also hear them referred to as *fixed-point* and *floating-point* values, respectively.

These names are derived from the way in which the computer stores the values and performs its arithmetic: floating-point arithmetic is a method of number manipulation used in computers to ease the problem of keeping track of the decimal point in involved arithmetic procedures and requires that the numbers be represented in a special form, whereas fixed-point numbers have a more simple representation and the decimal point is assumed to be in the same place – often at the right-hand end of the number – throughout the calculation. Floating-point arithmetic is of great importance; let us look at it a little more closely.

The first thing you must realise is that the size of numbers that can normally be represented inside a computer is limited, since there is a physical limit on the length of the registers in which the numbers are held while they are being processed. If you have a calculator, you will know that the same applies; eight digits is often the most that can be displayed. This limitation on the size of numbers leads to immediate difficulties.

Consider the case of a computer whose *word length* (the normal maximum number of digits in a register) is eight decimal digits, and let us attempt to multiply together the numbers 210 000 and 120 000 – both of which are easily accommodated. The result is 25 200 000 000, as a quick check with pencil and paper will show.

This turns out to be a bit inconvenient; the answer has 11 digits, but our machine can only hold eight! What can we do about it? One approach would be to re-examine the way in which we represent our numbers. Can we do it more economically and still get meaningful results? Suppose we rewrite 210 000 as $0.21 \times 1\,000\,000$, and 120 000 as $0.12 \times 1\,000\,000$. We can abbreviate these to $0.21 \times 10^6$ and $0.12 \times 10^6$, respectively. There are many other possibilities – $21 \times 10^4$, for instance, or $1200 \times 10^2$ – but it is found in practice that the greatest precision is maintained during the arithmetic processes if the *mantissa* (that part of the number which has to be multiplied by a power of 10) is a fraction between 0 and 1. The power of 10 by which the mantissa is multiplied is called the *exponent*, and together the mantissa and exponent constitute a floating-point number.

In FORTRAN, the number $0.21 \times 10^6$ would be written as 0.21E6, where 'E' stands for '$\times 10$' and the exponent, '6', is written *on* the line rather than above it, since the equipment used in the preparation of programs for input to a computer usually has no means of representing superscripts (or subscripts). This problem has to be overcome by the use of special symbols, and 'E' is one of these.

Now try writing the answer, 25 200 000 000, in this new way, without looking at the solution below.

Did you get $0.252 \times 10^{11}$? The FORTRAN representation would be 0.252E11. If you had the simpler version 0.252E11, this would be just as good, as would 2.52E10 (my calculator gives this), or any of the many other possibilities. 0.252 now fits easily into the eight-digit positions of a register, and so will the exponent, 11.

When writing FORTRAN, you may represent numbers in their familiar decimal form (but you must not forget the decimal point), or you may use the floating-point form; both ways are quite acceptable. The floating-point form (also called the *exponential* form) is perhaps best reserved for very large and very small numbers.

Numbers tend to be rather more complicated than the simple examples that have been quoted so far. One has to deal with negative values and small fractions, which implies that either or both the mantissa and the exponent of a floating-point number may be negative. This is indicated by preceding it by a minus sign $(-)$. Also, if it is felt that its use will clarify the meaning, positive values may be preceded by a plus sign (+). But values are taken to be positive unless a minus sign precedes them.

For example, −2970.34 is expressed in floating-point form as −.297034E+4; the first minus sign indicates that the number as a whole is negative, and the plus sign in the middle indicates that the mantissa is to be multiplied by a positive power of 10. But, in practice, the plus sign would normally be omitted, thus:

−.297034E4

Here is another example: 0.0316 expressed in exponential form.

0.0316 = +.316E−1

This means that 10 has to be raised to a negative power – the exponent is negative. In other words, we are to *divide* by the power of 10 rather than multiply by it. A list of numbers and the corresponding exponential forms is given below. Check each example carefully, and the principles of floating-point representation should quickly become clear.

```
   916.8 =   .9168E3
  −.9168 = −.9168E0
−.009168 = −.9168E−2
  9168.0 =   .9168E4
```

Generally, you will use the more familiar number representations, but the exponential form is useful when dealing with very large or very small numbers: .562E21 is a lot easier to write than

562000000000000000000.0

and similarly .2365E−15 is much easier to write, *and less error prone*, than

0.000000000000000002365

Floating-point notation can be used to represent very large numbers indeed (and very small ones, too). For example, 0.99E99 represents the digits 99 followed by 97 zeros – an enormous number. But the computer registers are still limited in size, and this will limit the number of significant figures that can be held in the floating-point mantissa. So this system does not necessarily give greater accuracy in our calculations and must be used with care.

However, the problems of keeping track of the decimal point are automated, thus simplifying the task of the programmer. As far as the examples in this book are concerned, the errors introduced when floating-point arithmetic is used are negligible, but you should be aware that such errors can arise.

One final point before we leave constants. It is quite normal for mathematicians and others to give *names* to constants. For instance, it is so much easier to write expressions in terms of $\pi$ ('pi') than to have to keep writing 3.14159; similarly, why keep writing 2.718281828 when the simple name 'e' can be – and usually is – used? FORTRAN 77 gives this ability. Consider the second line of the little program with which this section began:

```
PARAMETER (PI = 3.14159)
```

This is a preliminary instruction to the compiler, saying in effect: 'Whenever you meet the symbol PI, treat it exactly as though it were the constant 3.14159.' Notice the form of this *statement*, which must be strictly adhered to. It consists of the word PARAMETER, followed by a list of equalities contained in parentheses. In this case, there is only one equality in the list, but we could have several. Here is another example:

```
PARAMETER (G = 32.2, E = 2.7182818, N = 250)
```

The effect of the PARAMETER statement is to name a *constant*. The value thus given may *not* be changed. This brings us to the consideration of *variables*, whose values *can* be changed.

## Variables

Let us have another look at our simple program. The key statement is that on the fourth line:

```
CIRC = 2 * PI * RADIUS
```

This is a FORTRAN equivalent of the mathematical formula

circumference $= 2 \times \pi \times$ radius

but you will notice certain differences: few data preparation devices have the multiplication symbol, so the character * is used instead; FORTRAN does not permit names of more than six characters, so 'circumference' has been reduced to CIRC (CIRCUM has already been used to name the program, in line 1). Also, we use only capital letters. 2 and PI, we have already seen, are constants. The value of the radius could be anything within reason, and the value of the circumference is entirely dependent on the value of the radius. Both are completely variable, so RADIUS and CIRC, which can take any value, are called FORTRAN *variables*. You have a considerable amount of freedom in making up names for variables, but there are rules. Read them carefully.

1 The name of a variable must begin with an alphabetic character. Only capital letters are available.
2 The number of characters in a name must not exceed six.
3 After the first character, subsequent characters may be letters or digits.
4 No other characters are permitted in a name: special characters such as '.', '+' or '*' are not allowed.
5 Some names have a special meaning, and should not, in general, be used as variable names. Examples are 'SQRT' and 'ABS': we shall meet these again later.

The following are examples of valid variable names:

A ALPHA Q294GH MEAN POUNDS WAGE GROSS K9 DRWHO KOUNT1

Some compilers allow you rather more freedom in choosing names – more characters per name or a wider choice of characters. However, the standard specifies a maximum length of six characters, and if you want to run your programs on several different machines, you would be advised not to exceed this value.

Just to emphasise the point, here are some examples of *invalid* variable names with the reasons why they are not acceptable:

VARIABLE – has more than six characters
11PLUS – first character is not alphabetic
F1.DAT – contains a non-alphanumeric* character ('.')
DABS – looks good and is quite likely to be accepted by the compiler. Nevertheless, it has a special function and its use as a variable name is probably best avoided.

---

* An *alphabetic* character is one of the letters A–Z. A *numeric* character is one of the digits 0–9. An *alphanumeric* character is either alphabetic or numeric.

## Types of variable

Just as there are REAL and INTEGER constants, so there are REAL and INTEGER variables. An integer variable is one that can take only whole number values (no decimal point), such as 20, −235 or 551551. Real values, such as −273.2, 0.3010 or 98.4 can be held only by real variables. So how can they be distinguished from one another?

One way is by an explicit declaration of the type of the variable, usually at the head of the program, after the PROGRAM statement. In our example, we could have introduced it like this:

```
PROGRAM CIRCUM
REAL RADIUS, CIRC
```

Integer variables can be declared similarly, using the word INTEGER at the beginning of the statement, followed by a list of the names of the integer variables, separated by commas.

The other way is *not* to declare the type of your variables, but to choose their names rather more carefully. Unless otherwise specified in a type declaration, any variable names beginning with one of the letters I, J, K, L, M or N will be assumed by the compiler to be of integer type. Any others will be assumed to be of real type. So, in our example, there is no need to declare the type of the variables, since they all fall into the default REAL category.

## Expressions and assignment

One way to instruct the computer, in FORTRAN, is by presenting the process as a formula. Our example

```
CIRC = 2 * PI * RADIUS
```

illustrates this type of statement, known as an *assignment* statement because it requires that the arithmetic *expression* on the right-hand side of the = sign be evaluated and that value is then assigned to the variable named on the left-hand side. We are saying, in effect. 'Multiply PI (i.e. 3.14159) by 2 and multiply whatever is contained in the variable called RADIUS by the result. Then assign the resulting value to the variable called CIRC.'

Expressions consist of variables and constants connected by *operators*; our example contains two constants (2, PI), one variable

(RADIUS) and two multiplication operators (*). An assignment must only have a single variable on the left-hand side (at this stage). It may *not* be an expression; if it were, it would not make sense. It is worth pointing out that, although it looks very much like an equation, an assignment statement is something rather different. A commonly encountered assignment is one that looks like this:

```
I = I + 1
```

As an equation, this is nonsense: try to solve it for I, and what do we get? I −I =1, i.e. 0 = 1. Rubbish!

But, of course, it is *not* an equation; it is an assignment of a value to the variable I. And the value is whatever value I has to start with, plus 1. So, if I were 6, for example, the effect would be to make I take the value 7: 6 + 1. A better name for '=' in such cases is the *assignment operator*. Forget about 'equals'; when you see the '=' character, read it as 'becomes', 'is replaced by' or 'is assigned the value of'.

In fact, it is rare that the same variable turns up on both sides of an assignment. Here are some examples of simple arithmetic assignments:

```
HEIGHT = 1.82
GROSS = NETT + DEDS
F = 1.8 * C + 32.0
S = U * T + 0.5 * F * T ** 2
```

Well, perhaps not *all* that simple. In the last example the '**' operator was introduced. This is the FORTRAN representation of exponentiation – raising to a power. T ** 2 is equivalent to $T^2$ in standard notation, 'T squared' or T * T. In the third example above, the formula is one that determines the Fahrenheit temperature corresponding to a given Celsius temperature, C. If C has the value 18.0, what will be that calculated for F? It will be 1.8 × 18.0 + 32.0, which is 64.4.

*Remember:* A = B + C is valid, but B + C = A is not. Be sure you do not make this very common beginner's error.

The FORTRAN arithmetic assignment is usually very similar to the algebraic formula from which it is derived, but, as we have seen in the case of exponentiation, it is sometimes necessary to make changes. Division is another operation in which this becomes necessary. Consider the formula

$$\text{AVRAGE} = \frac{x1 + x2 + x3}{3.0}.$$

It cannot be written like that in FORTRAN. It has to be all on one line, like this, using '/' for the division operator:

```
AVRGE = (X1 + X2 + X3) / 3.0
```

Note how, to ensure that there is no doubt about what is to be 'above the line', it was necessary to enclose the sum in parentheses. Without them, the statement would be

```
AVRAGE = X1 + X2 + X3 / 3.0
```

but this is equivalent to a different formula:

$$\text{AVRAGE} = x1 + x2 + \frac{x3}{3.0}.$$

Here, only the last term, x3, is divided by 3.0, whereas we really want the sum of three terms on top. So we do need those parentheses here and in any other place where we want to make the meaning of an expression quite clear and unambiguous.

## Evaluation of expressions

We have now met all the arithmetic operators:

| add | + |
| subtract | − |
| multiply | * |
| divide | / |
| exponentiate | ** |

We have also seen that parentheses, ( and ), can be used to clarify the meaning of expressions. There are rules that specify the order in which the operations are applied and some restrictions as to the way in which they are applied; these will now be summarised.

1 Expressions in parentheses are evaluated before any others.
2 The arithmetic operators are applied in the order

first, **
then, * and /
finally, + and −

3 It is not permitted to have two arithmetic operators adjacent.
4 The divide(/) operator has some rather special properties if its operands are both of *integer* type; the result of the division is itself an integer – the normal result truncated (cut off) at the decimal point.

**Examples**

We have already seen an example of the application of rule 1, in the calculation of AVRAGE, above. To evaluate the expression:

$\dfrac{a + b}{c + d}$ we should have to write (A + B) / (C + D).

Failure to use parentheses would be interpreted as something quite different:

A + B / C + D is equivalent to $a + \dfrac{b}{c} + d$

The golden rule is: *if in doubt, use parentheses*. It makes little difference to the time it takes to write or run your program and you can be sure of removing any possibility of misinterpretation. Better to overparenthesise than not to use enough.

Although it is quite usual to omit the multiplication operator when writing mathematical expressions, this is not permitted in FORTRAN. Where you might normally write, for example, $a(b + c)$, your FORTRAN expression must be A * (B + C). This is a common early error – avoid it.

Rule 3 means that you may not have an expression such as E ** − (K * T), which brings ** and − operators together. Rephrase it as E ** (−(K * T)) or E ** (−K * T).

If there is a sequence of similar operations, + and − or * and / , these are evaluated in order from left to right. So the FORTRAN expression

```
A * X ** 2 + B * X ** 3 − C * X **4
```

will be evaluated by

1 Form $x^2$ and multiply by A.
2 Form $x^3$ and multiply by B.
3 Add the results of steps 1 and 2 to give $AX^2 + BX^3$.
4 Form $x^4$ and multiply by C.
5 Subtract this from the result at step 3, giving $AX^2 + BX^3 − CX^4$.

Integer division is a process that some people find surprising, but you will get some unexpected results if you do not appreciate the sort of answers it can produce. Results of dividing one INTEGER quantity – constant or variable – by another are themselves of INTEGER type. But integers are whole numbers, with no fraction part; if the division might be expected to give a fraction part in the answer, that part has to be lost. This is achieved by simply cutting the number off at the decimal point. So a result of 3.142 would become 3, −22.4 would become −22; a result between 0 and 1, such as 0.456 or even 0.99999999 is reduced to 0 – this can be quite a shock if you are unprepared for it. Here are some FORTRAN divisions involving both REAL and INTEGER quantities, with an indication of the results that will be obtained. Notice that if any of the operands (values being manipulated) in a division are of REAL type, the result will also be real; integers are converted to real values, just for the purpose of calculation. We assume that A = 3.0, B = 4.0, I = 3, J = 4

| Expression | Value |
|------------|-----------|
| A/B | 0.75 |
| A/J | 0.75 |
| I/B | 0.75 |
| I/J | 0 |
| B/I | 1.3333333 |
| J/I | 1 |

## A little more about exponentiation

Exponentiation is the process of raising a number to a power. When we multiply a number by itself, we say we have raised it to the power of 2, or *squared* it: $a \times a = a^2$. If we now multiply this by $a$ again, we shall have raised $a$ to the power 3, or *cubed* it; we write the result as $a^3$. In general, $a^n$ is said to be the $n$th power of $a$ and represents the number $a \times a \times a \times \ldots$ in which $a$ appears $n$ times. The figure written above the line, specifying the power to which the number has been raised, is called the *exponent*. It is usually a whole number, but it does not have to be; $p^{5/2}$ is an alternative way of writing $\sqrt{p^5}$, and might equally well have been written as $p^{2.5}$.

In FORTRAN, since we cannot use superscripts, we should have to express these values as P ** (5.0/2.0) or, preferably, P ** 2.5. Note that, because of the integer division feature already mentioned, P ** (5/2) would not give us what we want; it would be equivalent to having written P ** 2.

You need to be a little bit careful in using the ** operator. An expression whose value is zero may not be raised to the power zero, or to a negative power ($a^{-n}$ is the same as $1/a^n$). An expression whose value is negative may not be raised to any real power – this avoids the problems that an expression such as $(-1.0)$ ** 0.5 might raise for the system. Generally speaking, if the exponent is a whole number, it is better to write it in its INTEGER form, since this will often lead to the production of more efficient code by the compiler.

One last point about exponentiation: if you have an expression such as 2 ** 3 ** 4, what is its value? It all depends which end you approach it from: left to right evaluation gives us (2 ** 3) ** 4, which is 8 ** 4, i.e. 4096; right to left evaluation gives us a different answer, 2 ** (3 ** 4), which is 2 ** 81 – an enormous value. FORTRAN 77 specifies quite clearly that in such a case evaluation is to be from RIGHT to LEFT, i.e. in this case the result would be $2^{81}$. Do it yourself.

You are now in a position to be able to write simple programs. The information you most need at this stage is how to get data into the computer and how to print your results. We have already seen a couple of example programs involving input and output, but the simple technique will be summarised here.

For *input*, use the READ * instruction, followed by a list of the variables to which the data values are to be given. You will have to supply those values at the time the program is running and bear in mind that the order of data items must correspond exactly to the order of the names in the READ statement. Here is an example:

```
READ *, A, B, SIZE, LENGTH, N
```

Notice that READ * is followed by a comma and the names of variables in the list are also separated from each other by commas. There is no comma after the last variable name. If the data presented to this program when it runs is this:

```
8.42,   98.4,   15.49,   27, 5
```

then we shall finish up by having allocated values as follows:

A $= 8.42$          B $= 98.4$
SIZE $= 15.49$      LENGTH $= 27$
N $= 5$

Note that commas are used to separate the data values. We could equally well have used spaces (blank characters). We shall stick to commas when giving examples in this book.

Similarly, for *output*, use the PRINT * instruction, followed by a list of the items to be printed. Here you have a little more flexibility, since you can use *character constants* to identify the items. An example follows.

The following program determines the total amount of simple interest on a loan amount *P* at a rate of interest *r* over a period of *t* years. The formula is $I = Prt/100$. The action of the program is almost self-evident, but *comment* lines have been introduced for explanation. In FORTRAN 77, a comment line is one which is completely blank, or has either a 'c' or a '*' in the first position of the line. Comments are ignored by the compiler, but help to make the program more intelligible for the human reader. You are urged to use them freely.

```
      PROGRAM INTRST
C     THIS PROGRAM READS IN THE PRINCIPAL AMOUNT, P,
C     THE PERCENTAGE RATE OF SIMPLE INTEREST, R,
C     AND THE NUMBER OF YEARS FOR WHICH THE MONEY IS
C     INVESTED, T. IT THEN CALCULATES THE TOTAL AMOUNT
C     OF INTEREST DUE, I, AND PRINTS ALL FOUR VALUES.
      REAL I
C     FIRST READ IN THE DATA VALUES
      READ *, P, R, T
C     NOW APPLY THE FORMULA
      I = (P * R * T) / 100
C     AND PRINT THE RESULT
      PRINT *, 'PRINCIPAL AMOUNT', P,
     +         'INTEREST RATE', R, '%'
      PRINT *, 'TIME INVESTED', T,
     +         'TOTAL INTEREST', I
      END
```

The way in which the data is supplied will vary from machine to machine. It may be on punched cards or paper tape, or you may be fortunate enough to be able to work *on-line* – sitting before a terminal device with a video screen on which your output is displayed and a keyboard which you use for input. You will have to find this out for yourself, as it applies to the equipment you will be using. Note the character constants in the example: each is a string of characters enclosed in single quotation marks, such as 'TOTAL INTEREST', and each – like a numeric constant – represents itself. So the output from the program will consist of the numeric values for P, R, T and I interspersed with appropriate text. Thus, given the following data set

200, 5.5, 7

(i.e. an amount of, say, £200 invested at 5½% simple for 7 years) the results should appear rather like this:

```
PRINCIPAL AMOUNT 200.0 INTEREST RATE 5.5 %
TIME INVESTED 7.0 TOTAL INTEREST 77.0
```

It is not possible to be more precise than this about the form of the output, since the standard leaves rather a lot of freedom to the writer of the compiler as to exactly how he deals with this type of output statement. Notice, however, that each PRINT statement starts a new line. This is the normal approach.

## Exercises

*Note:* Wherever possible, write programs and run them.

1 What will be the numerical result of executing the following FORTRAN sequences?

(a)  ```
     A = 3.0
     F9 = A ** 2 + 3.46
     ```

   Determine the value of F9.

(b)  ```
     W = 1.25
     P = 5 * (W/5 + 1)
     ```

   What is the value of P?

(c)  ```
     NUMBER = 4
     ALPHA = NUMBER ** 3
     ```

   What is the value of ALPHA?

2 The following is the specification for a calculation, for which an assignment is to be written. Below it are a number of statements. State which of these statements are *wrong*, and give your reasons.
     ```

'Subtract 3.9 from the variable A, and raise the difference to the power 3. Multiply the result by B and divide by 5.6. Assign the result to the variable BETA.'

```
(a)  BETA = (A − 3.9) ** 3 * B / 5.6
(b)  BETA = (3.9 − A) ** 3 * B / 5.6
(c)  BETA = (A − 3.9) * B ** 3 / 5.6
(d)  BETA = B * (A − 3.9) ** 3 / 5.6
(e)  (A − 3.9) ** 3 * B / 5.6 = BETA
(f)  BETA = B / 5.6 * (A − 3.9) ** 3
(g)  BETA = A − 3.9 ** 3 * B / 5.6
```

3 Write a complete FORTRAN 77 program to input data and print the value of the following formula:

$$E = \frac{3.479\ dp^2}{5.67 + Q}$$

4 Write a FORTRAN statement for the following formula:

$$y = 8x^3 + 7x + 4.3x^2$$

5 Can you see a way of rearranging the formula of question 4 so as to give a quite different FORTRAN statement which produces the same answer?

6 Evaluate the following FORTRAN expressions:

(a)  `J * (K − 2 * L) / 6 + J ** 2`

   where $J = 2$, $K = 10$, $L = 2$

(b)  `4 * (B / 2.5 * C) ** 2 + 3`

   where $B = 10.0$, $C = 2.0$

(c)  `4 * (B / (2.5 * C)) ** 2 + 3`

   where $B = 10.0$, $C = 2.0$

(d)  `(F * (F − G)) / (V − 3.5)`

   where $F = -5.0$, $G = -3.0$, $V = 5.5$

(e)  `A ** B ** C`

   where $A = 4$, $B = 3$, $C = 2$

(f)  `A * B / C ** D`

   where $A = 1.0$, $B = 4.0$, $C = 4.0$, $D = 2.0$

# 4

# Oddments

We have briefly mentioned the media which may be used to present data and programs to the computer. The original FORTRAN language was designed around what was then, in the USA, the principal means of input to the computer – the punched card. It remains a largely card-oriented language, and it is time we considered this aspect in a little more detail.

Although recent work is encouraging, there is still no readily available equipment that will read normal handwritten material directly into the memory of the computer. Nor, except in a very restricted sense, is the direct input of human speech possible. Consequently, we find it necessary to encode the information we wish to present to the computer – whether it be programs or data – in such a way that it can be interpreted by electromechanical devices. Today it is possible to do this in a number of ways, one of the most popular being to accept characters as they are typed at the keyboard of a visual display unit, looking rather like a TV set with a keyboard; these characters are then stored either in the main memory of the machine or on some magnetic backing storage medium, such as magnetic tape or magnetic disc, in one of its several forms. Still very popular, however, is the punched card reader, whose medium is the 80-column punched card, originally developed by Hollerith in the late nineteenth century. A card is capable of holding 80 characters of information, each represented by a unique pattern of holes in one of the columns of the card. These patterns are punched automatically when the corresponding character is typed on a machine called a *keypunch*, which is equipped with a more or less standard typewriter keyboard.

The card itself is thin, normally $7\frac{3}{8} \times 3\frac{1}{4}$ inches, with one corner cut off to facilitate the stacking of a *deck* (or *pack*) of cards so that they are all the same way up. The cards are read into computer memory by a *card reader*, which converts the unique hole patterns into equally unique electronic signals that can be stored to represent the corresponding characters. Many keypunch machines have a printing option, so that the information punched into a card is also printed along the top edge, making it easy to see what the card contains.

Fig. 4.1 is a picture of a typical punched card. The left-most column is designated column 1 and the right-most is column 80. You will see that each column contains 12 rows, 10 numbered 0 to 9 and two others in the wide top margin. These last two are known by a number of different names, depending on whose equipment you are using; the top hole may be variously called the 12, + or R punch, the second is the 11, – or X punch. There are even some who refer to them as the 11 and 10 punches respectively, which seems to have a certain amount of logic in it.

Numeric characters are represented by a single hole; to punch.the character '7' in column 29, a hole is punched at the intersection of row 7 and column 29. Alphabetic information requires that we punch more than one hole in a column; thus, the letter 'A' has a '12–1' punch – holes in the 12 row and also the 1 row in the same column. For special characters, it may be felt necessary to punch up to three holes in a column, but more than this is rarely encountered.

Once the program has been written, the actual punching of the cards is performed as a clerical operation by keypunch operators who know, generally speaking, little about programming. It is very important, therefore, that all work to be keypunched should be clearly written so that transcription errors do not occur at this stage. The finished cards should also be checked visually after punching to ensure that there are no errors that will be passed onto the computer. Such checks, though tedious, can save a lot of expensive computer time. To aid this process, even if the keypunch does not print the characters along the top of the card, there are other machines called *interpreters*, which will add the printed annotation after the cards have been punched.

The cards for important data and programs are usually checked

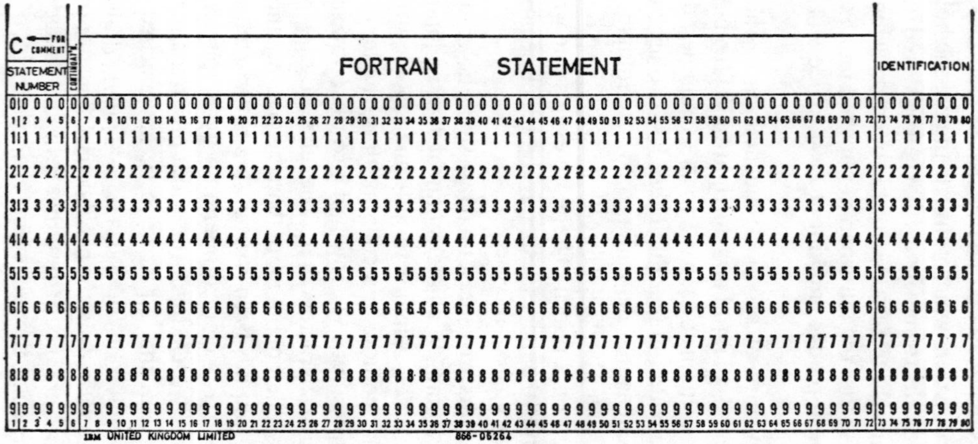
C ← FOR COMMENT
STATEMENT NUMBER
CONTINUAT'N.
FORTRAN STATEMENT
IDENTIFICATION
IBM UNITED KINGDOM LIMITED
866-05264

Fig. 4.1

by a process called *verification*. The machine used, called a *verifier*, looks like a keypunch and is used in much the same way. However, the cards fed into it have already been punched. The operator goes through the motions of repunching the card deck, and if what she punches differs from that which is already punched on the card then the machine will warn her that an error has occurred, by flashing a light, for instance, and jamming the keyboard. The card being verified can now be examined more closely and be repunched if it turns out to be in error. Verification should be performed by an operator different from the one who punched the original deck of cards, if possible, to avoid the possibility that she might repeat her own errors. Even so, errors do creep through and an eye check should be performed whenever possible. If a card is found to be wrong, it is usually difficult and uneconomical to correct it and so it will usually be repunched *and reverified*.

## The FORTRAN statement

A FORTRAN statement is, broadly, an instruction. It is either an instruction that will be obeyed at runtime or information for the compiler that will be used at compile time. It generally embraces much more than a machine-language instruction. In flowchart terms, the effect of a single box, or even several boxes, may be achieved with one FORTRAN statement. Thus, one might have a box that contains the order: 'Set COUNT to zero'. As a FORTRAN statement, this would probably be written as:

```
COUNT = 0
```

This is an example, as we have already seen, of an arithmetic assignment statement. Another statement would probably be required at an earlier stage:

```
INTEGER COUNT
```

specifying that COUNT, although it does not conform to the naming convention for integers, nevertheless is to be treated as an INTEGER variable. This is information the *compiler* will need to generate the correct sequence of object code when processing COUNT. The statement is a member of a whole family of *specification* statements, which give instructions to the compiler about such matters as the organisation of memory that will be necessary when the program is finally executed. They are known as *non-executable* statements, for their prime function is organisational, whereas those which perform the actual calculations and other manipulations of data are known as *executable* statements. It is quite important to distinguish between the two; a flowchart describing the process for which a program is to be written would not normally show any actions corresponding to the non-executable statements.

FORTRAN was originally designed in terms of statements punched into 80-column cards. Fig. 4.2 shows the way in which the columns of the standard punched card are allocated to the various parts of the FORTRAN statement. Often, a computer installation will supply specially printed cards for FORTRAN programs, which may have the words FORTRAN STATEMENT printed across the top. However, it does not matter what is printed on the card – the information is contained in the holes. What *is* important is the positioning of the information on the card. If statements are not positioned exactly, even though they may be syntactically correct,

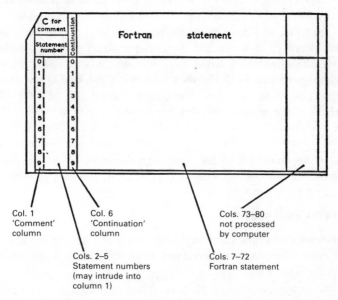

Col. 1
'Comment'
column

Col. 6
'Continuation'
column

Cols. 73–80
not processed
by computer

Cols. 2–5
Statement numbers
(may intrude into
column 1)

Cols. 7–72
Fortran statement

**Fig. 4.2**

the compiler will usually report that the statement – or even its predecessor – has an error. This is because certain constituents of the statement are expected to be in specific places on the card, and most compilers are not sufficiently flexible in their analysis to be able to allow for slight divergences from this expectation. In this way, we get fast and efficient compilers. More flexibility would slow things down, the originators of the language seem to have thought, and they may well have been right in 1958. Today there are a number of computer systems whose FORTRAN compilers are more tolerant – but they do not conform to the standard, which specifies a fixed statement format.

A statement usually occupies a single card, but it may extend across several. Thus statements are said to have an *initial* (first) line and *continuation* lines; if a statement is too long to be completely accommodated on its initial line, it overflows onto as many continuation lines as may be necessary.* In normal circumstances, column 6 is not used. If it contains anything other than zero (0) or a blank character, it marks a continuation line. In such a case, columns 1 to 5 must be blank.

```
   PRINT *,
1            X,
2            Y,
3            Z
```

The above is an example of a PRINT statement, deliberately spread over a total of four lines to show how continuation is achieved. Note that any character in column 6 serves to indicate a continuation line, except '0' or a blank: it is quite common, as here, to number the lines in column 6.

It is *not* permitted, by the way, for more than one statement to share a line. This applies even when the statements are very short, wasteful though it may seem.

## Column 1

This is the *comment* column, briefly mentioned in the previous chapter. It will normally be blank, but it may contain the letter 'C'

---

* The FORTRAN 77 standard actually specifies a maximum of 19 continuation lines. It seems very unlikely that this number would ever be needed, in practice.

or an asterisk. If it does, this is an indication from the programmer to the compiler that the contents of this card constitute a comment – descriptive information about the program, designed to help those who read it to understand its construction better. Such information will appear in the *program listing* (the printout of the program normally produced when it is compiled), but will be ignored by the compiler. This is an extremely useful feature.

## Columns 2 to 5

This set of columns, usually termed the *statement number field*, will generally be blank, but it may contain a number.

When a program has a point at which a decision is made, it will often happen that a set of FORTRAN statements has to be executed in an order other than that in which they appear in the listing. Or, as in the first complete program example in Chapter 1, it may be required that a group of statements should be repeated in a loop. In such cases, it is necessary to branch from one statement to another that does not follow it in the normal written sequence. This implies that statements can be identified by some means, so that the statement that initiates a branch can specify the exact whereabouts of the next statement to be executed. The way this is achieved is by allocating a *statement number* to the 'target' statement and writing it in the statement number field. Thus one might write GO TO 29 in a program; when executed the effect would be for the statement labelled '29' to be the next one executed. This is called a program *branch*.

It is not necessary to number all statements, nor is it desirable. Statements are numbered – or *labelled* – to clarify the flow of a program. If all statements are labelled, this aim is not going to be achieved. Only those statements that are referenced by other statements need to be labelled.

All statement numbers should be different and should, preferably be sequential; though this is not required, it makes the program easier to follow. The first statement of a program could be labelled 2034, while a later one had the label 27. This is correct, but not recommended. It would, however, be quite wrong and unacceptable to the compiler if there were two statements in the program labelled 2034.

The range of acceptable statement numbers is from 1 to 99999, always integers, never negative. Five-digit statement numbers should have the first digit in column 1. Imbedded spaces are ignored.

## The statement body

The main body of the statement will be contained between columns 7 and 72, inclusive of the initial line and as many continuation lines as may be needed. Most statements will fit comfortably onto one card, but the continuation feature may have to be used occasionally. Spaces may be used quite freely to improve the readability of your *program* statements. This does not normally apply to the data, whose format is usually strictly prescribed.

## Summary

1 Column 1 is used to identify comments and may also hold the first digit of a statement number.
2 Columns 2 to 5 are used solely for statement numbers and will be blank if the statement is not labelled. Only those statements that are referred to by others need be numbered. The statement number may appear anywhere within the statement number field – there is no need to align all statement numbers on the left or right of the field, though the appearance and readability of the program are improved if this is done.
3 Column 6 is the continuation column. If a card is used for continuing the statement from the preceding card, it should have a non-zero, non-blank character in column 6.
4 Finally, columns 73 to 80 are not used by the FORTRAN compiler and may be used by the programmer for any purpose. It is usual to put sequence numbers in this field, in case the card deck is accidentally mixed up.

Now try the following short test. All the answers will be found in the preceding section.

1 How many columns are there in the standard punched card?
2 How many of these are used by the FORTRAN compiler?

3 What is the maximum number of statements you can place on a single card?

4 How many characters may be punched in a single column? How many holes?

5 If a statement were too long to fit on to one card, what would you do?

6 Some of the following statements are true, others are false. Which is which? When you decide that a statement is false, give your reasons. The answers are given after the last statement.
   (a) A FORTRAN statement starts in column 1.
   (b) Column 1 is used to contain either the first digit of a statement number or a comment indicator.
   (c) All statements should be numbered.
   (d) A FORTRAN statement extends from column 7 to column 80.
   (e) Column 6 is the continuation column.
   (f) Spaces may not be left between FORTRAN characters.
   (g) Each character must have a column to itself.
   (h) FORTRAN statements always start in column 7.
   (i) Small (lower case) letters may be used in FORTRAN.
   (j) The identification field (columns 73 to 80) must not be left blank.

## Answers to question 6

(a) False. A statement may start anywhere on the card, other than column 6 or beyond column 72. If it is numbered, the statement number must appear between columns 1 and 5, inclusive. If it is not, the first character must appear between columns 7 and 72, inclusive.

(b) False. A statement intended as a comment will certainly contain either the letter 'C' or an asterisk (' * ') in column 1, but the first digit of a statement number need not, necessarily, appear in that position on the card. If the statement number has five digits, the first digit *must* be in column 1.

(c) False – only those which are referred to elsewhere.

(d) False. It must not extend beyond column 72, and the statement number may start as early as column 1.

(e) True. This is where the continuation indicator is placed.

(f) False. Spaces may be freely used to improve readability.
(g) True. It is not possible to punch more than one legible character in one column position. Try it and see!
(h) False. See comments on 6(a) and 6(d).
(i) False – up to a point. When writing normal instructions, you must use capital letters. However, depending on the compiler you use, it may be possible to include lower-case characters in character constants. You will have to check this for yourself.
(j) False. Columns 73 to 80 may contain anything. It makes sense to use them for sequence numbers, especially in large program decks.

Finally, a few remarks on the handling of punched cards might be appropriate here. Modern punched card machinery is very good and some readers can cope with cards that have been incredibly badly handled. Even so, it is as well to look after your card decks and try to keep them in good condition. When carrying and manipulating cards, always be careful not to damage their edges. They should be stored in a dry and dust-free place. When the cards are read by machine, each card is usually read twice and the card will be rejected if the second reading differs from the first. A typical reason for this is that the keypunch has produced holes slightly out of alignment, in which case the punch will need attention.

# 5

# Decisions and branches

You can now write very simple programs, but they have very little practical use. This is because you do not yet know how to harness the computer in such a way that it can decide for itself which of several possible logical paths to take when such a decision has to be made. This situation occurs frequently, and it is time we had a look at how FORTRAN tackles it.

## Decisions, decisions!

The chief decision mechanism of FORTRAN 77 is the IF statement, which enables the program to proceed via either one group of statements or another. Which group is chosen to be executed depends on the result of testing a *condition*. For this reason, it is often referred to as a *conditional branch*. In effect, the program branches in two (sometimes more) directions, and the condition test determines which of these branches is to be taken. In particular, the FORTRAN 77 'block IF' statement is designed to ensure that, whichever branch is taken, the two will normally converge again into a common path. This makes the program easier to understand and to design. Fig. 5.1 shows, in flowchart terms, the structure of the block IF statement.

A typical block IF statement might look like this:

```
IF (B**2 — 4*A*C .GE. 0) THEN
    PRINT *, 'REAL ROOTS'
ELSE
    PRINT *, 'COMPLEX ROOTS'
END IF
```

and its flowchart is given in Fig. 5.2

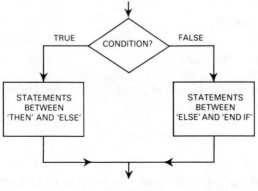

**Fig. 5.1**

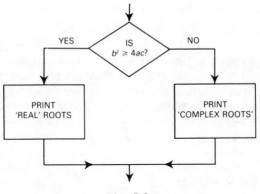

**Fig. 5.2**

Before we proceed much further, however, we must look more closely at these conditions.

## Relations

The 'condition' being tested is often the very simple one of the relationship between two quantities. For numeric values, there are six such relations, but FORTRAN – because of the limitations of the keypunch keyboard – does not use the normal mathematical symbols for them. They are shown in the following table.

| *Mathematical symbol* | *Meaning* | *FORTRAN symbol* |
|---|---|---|
| $<$ | less than | .LT. |
| $\leqslant$ | less than or equal to | .LE. |
| $=$ | equal to | .EQ. |
| $\neq$ | not equal to | .NE. |
| $\geqslant$ | greater than or equal to | .GE. |
| $>$ | greater than | .GT. |

The full stops (periods) before and after the letters of the FORTRAN symbols are important. They serve to distinguish these *relational operators* from ordinary variable names and *must not be omitted*.

You will now see how it is that, in our example, $b^2 - 4ac \geqslant 0$ comes to be rendered as

```
B**2 — 4*A*C .GE. 0.
```

Relational operators are used to form relational expressions. It is surprising, at first, to realise that such expressions – no matter how involved the arithmetic expressions they contain – always evaluate to one of only two possible values: *true*, or *false*. In this respect, they form a subset of the *logical expressions*, which all evaluate to either true or false.

## Logical expressions

The values 'true' and 'false' can be represented and stored in a computer memory in much the same way as we can store numerical and character values. They are, however, held in memory locations specifically reserved for the purpose.

There are two logical constants: .TRUE. and .FALSE. As in the case of the relational operators, they are delimited (i.e. preceded and followed) by periods.

We may also have logical variables – those that can only take the values .TRUE. and .FALSE. Such variables must have appeared in a type-declaration statement at the head of the *program unit* (this term is defined more fully later, but at the moment may be taken to be synonymous with program) in which they are used.

For example, the variable LIGHT would normally, because its first letter is 'l', be of INTEGER type. To make it into a variable of LOGICAL type, we have to declare it early in the program unit, thus:

```
LOGICAL LIGHT
```

After this, we may assign logical values to it, either directly:

```
LIGHT = .TRUE.
```

or through the evaluation of a logical expression:

```
LIGHT = LAMP .EQ. 1
```

In the first case, LIGHT is assigned the value of the logical constant .TRUE. In the second, the logical expression LAMP .EQ. 1 is evaluated; if LAMP has the value of 1, this expression has the value .TRUE., otherwise its value is .FALSE. Whatever it is, that value is assigned to the logical variable LIGHT.

## Logical operators

Just as we need arithmetic operators like + and * to form useful arithmetic expressions, we have three *logical operators* that enable us to form more complex logical expressions. These operators are .NOT., .OR. and .AND. Again, the period delimiters are important!

The .NOT. operator has the effect of reversing the value of a logical item from true to false, or vice versa. Thus, .NOT. .TRUE. is the same as .FALSE. and, similarly, .NOT. .FALSE. is the same as .TRUE. More usefully, if A is a logical variable then .NOT. A has the value

.FALSE. if A is .TRUE.

or

.TRUE. if A is .FALSE.

We can summarise this in a *truth table*, in which the letters T and F are used to represent .TRUE. and .FALSE., respectively. It looks like this:

| A | .NOT. A |
|---|---------|
| F | T |
| T | F |

The .OR. operator acts on *two* logical expressions. A .OR. B is .TRUE. if *either* A *or* B (or both) is .TRUE. Here it is in truth table form:

| A | B | A .OR. B |
|---|---|----------|
| F | F | F |
| F | T | T |
| T | F | T |
| T | T | T |

The .AND. operator also requires two logical expressions to work on. A .AND. B is .TRUE. only if *both* A *and* B are .TRUE. The truth table is:

| A | B | A .AND. B |
|---|---|-----------|
| F | F | F |
| F | T | F |
| T | F | F |
| T | T | T |

In just the same way as arithmetic operators, these logical operators are applied with a specific order of precedence: first, .NOT., then .AND. and, finally, .OR. Parentheses can be used to change this order, if necessary, because expressions in parenthesis are evaluated first, as usual.

Logical operators are applied *after* the arithmetic operators and relational operators have been dealt with. So the expression

```
A .LT. 0 .AND. P .NE. Q + 3.2
```

will be evaluated as though it were

```
(A .LT. 0) .AND. (P .NE. (Q + 3.2))
```

This ensures that we first perform the addition to produce a numerical value, then the two relational expressions are evaluated, each producing a logical result, .TRUE. or .FALSE.; finally, the .AND. operator acts on these to produce the result, .TRUE. or .FALSE. You must remember these operator precedences:

1 ARITHMETIC
  (a) **
  (b) * and /
  (c) + and −
2 RELATIONAL
  .LT., .LE., .EQ., .NE., .GE. and .GT.
  All are of equal priority.
3 LOGICAL
  (a) .NOT.
  (b) .AND.
  (c) .OR.

We can now make our logical expressions – and hence the conditions being tested in our IF statements – as complicated as we wish. It is usually wise to resist this temptation and aim for simplicity, as far as possible!

Sometimes, however, it is useful to be able to express a complex set of conditions with a relatively simple and readable logical expression.

**Example**
In general, a leap year is one in which the year number is exactly divisible by four. This does not apply in the case of century years, however, unless they are also divisible by 400. Thus, 1984 is a leap year, but 1900 was not; 2000 will be a leap year.

One problem here is that of determining the remainder when one number is divided by another. For two integers I and J, the remainder when I is divided by J is given by the expression $I - (I/J)*J$. Remember that when a division involves only integers, the result is also an integer which is the truncated quotient. Now we can write the required logical expression; let LEAP be a variable of LOGICAL type, YEAR an INTEGER.

```
  LEAP = YEAR — (YEAR/100)*100 .NE. 0
*     .AND. YEAR — (YEAR/4  )*  4 .EQ. 0
      .OR.  YEAR — (YEAR/100)*100 .EQ. 0
      .AND. YEAR — (YEAR/400)*400 .EQ. 0
```

If YEAR represents a leap year, LEAP will be set .TRUE.; if not, the final value of LEAP will be .FALSE.

There are several other ways in which this calculation can be performed. Some would say, for instance, that it is wasteful to have the arithmetic expression for deciding whether the year is a century year or not appear twice. Indeed, one could go further – at the expense of introducing new logical variables R4, R100, and R400 – and produce something that is more readable:

```
R4   = YEAR — (YEAR/ 4 )* 4  .EQ. 0
R100 = YEAR — (YEAR/100)*100 .EQ. 0
R400 = YEAR — (YEAR/400)*400 .EQ. 0
LEAP = .NOT. R100 .AND. R4
  .OR.         R100 .AND. R400
```

We get even more readability if we make use of one of the *intrinsic functions* which FORTRAN makes available to its users. There are a number of these, which will be dealt with at a later stage; suffice it to say that the expression MOD(I,J) is completely equivalent to (and much less tedious to write than) $I - (I/J)*J$. Thus the expression simplifies to

```
 LEAP = MOD(YEAR, 100) .NE. 0 .AND.
*         MOD(YEAR,   4) .EQ. 0
*.OR.     MOD(YEAR, 100) .EQ. 0 .AND.
*         MOD(YEAR, 400) .EQ. 0
```

Another way would be to define the logical variable CNTURY:

```
CNTURY = MOD(YEAR, 100) .EQ. 0
```

and then write

```
LEAP = .NOT. CNTURY .AND. MOD(YEAR, 4) .EQ. 0
  .OR.       CNTURY .AND. MOD(YEAR, 400) .EQ. 0
```

After a little practice, handling such expressions becomes almost second nature, but many people dislike doing so. An alternative, often, is to use an IF statement.

## The IF statement

This takes the general form shown below.

```
IF condition THEN
    group of statements to be executed
    if the condition is true
ELSE
    group of statements to be executed
```

if the condition is false
END IF

There are several types of IF statement. This is the most general, called the 'block IF' statement.

The simplest application of the block IF statement is that in which we consider the prevailing conditions and choose either to take a particular action or not. Thus, in everyday terms, we might have a rule such as:

*If* the weather forecast is 'rainy' *then*
  carry a raincoat.

No alternative is specified, or needed – we assume that if it is not rainy the instruction to carry a raincoat will be ignored.

In a similar way, the block IF statement can be shortened by omitting the ELSE part:

```
IF (LEAP) THEN
  YRDAYS = YRDAYS + 1
  FEB    = 29
  SHEMAY = .TRUE.
END IF
```

Do not forget the END IF; without it, the compiler cannot determine how many statements depend upon the truth of the given condition.

Taking things a stage further, when there is a well-defined alternative course of action, we use the ELSE clause:

*If* the car is OK *then*
  load up the picnic hamper;
  check the route;
  pick up the girl friend;
  drive to the sea.
*Else*
  ring the girl friend;
  explain the problem;
  arrange to meet for lunch in town.

In the following FORTRAN example, we have a common stock control situation. When an order comes in, we need to decide whether or not it can be met from existing stocks. If not, some action needs to be taken to alert the warehouse staff. If the order can be met, stock levels need to be adjusted appropriately.

```
IF (STOCK .GT. MIN) THEN
   STOCK = STOCK - ORDER
   CUST  = CUST + ORDER
   PRINT *, 'CUSTOMER: ', CUSTNO, ' ORDER MET'
ELSE
   PRINT *, 'LOW STOCK: ', CUSTNO
END IF
```

Remember to enclose the condition in parentheses!

One or more block IFs can be nested inside one another. This may occur in either the THEN or the ELSE clause, or even in both:

*If* there is enough dry wood *then*
   *If* the fireplace is not cleaned out *then*
      clean out the fireplace;
      lay the fire;
      light the fire.
*Else*
   use the electric fire;
   order some more dry wood.

Sequence checks are quite important in many data processing applications. In the following FORTRAN 77 examples, three variables A, B and C are compared to determine whether or not they form an ascending sequence of values.

```
IF (A .LT. B) THEN
   IF (B .LT. C) THEN
     PRINT *, 'OK'
   ELSE
     PRINT *, 'SEQUENCE ERROR'
   END IF
ELSE
   PRINT *, 'SEQUENCE ERROR'
END IF
```

Personally, I do not like this – there is unnecessary duplication. An alternative might be:

```
IF (A .LT. B) THEN
   IF (B .LT. C) THEN
     PRINT *, 'OK'
   END IF
ELSE
   PRINT *, 'SEQUENCE ERROR'
END IF
```

Or might it? If you look carefully, you will see that when A is less than B but B is not less than C, nothing is printed. So this is not an acceptable alternative. But there is an even simpler possibility:

```
IF (A .LT. B .AND. B .LT. C) THEN
   PRINT *, 'OK'
ELSE
   PRINT *, 'SEQUENCE ERROR'
END IF
```

The moral is: Look for the simple solution. 'THEN IF . . .' constructions may be confusing; avoid them if you can.

Strangely (it is all to do with how much information the mind can stack up before making use of the first item) nesting IFs after ELSE is not nearly so confusing. Here we are stating a series of conditions and, immediately, the action to be taken in each case. Like this:

check fishing tackle;
*If* the weather is fine *then*
   head for the river
*Else*
   *If* it is snowing *then*
      stay in bed
   *Else*
      *If* there was a frost last night *then*
         stay home and fix broken windows
   *Else*
      head for the lake.

A FORTRAN example follows. A number N is read, whose value determines whether or not another number is wanted. If the second value is read, its value determines the further action to be taken.

```
READ *, N
IF (N .LT. 0) THEN
   PRINT *, 'END OF FILE'
ELSE
   READ *, X
   SUM = SUM + X
   IF (SUM .GT. MAX) THEN
      ALARM = .TRUE.
      SUM = SUM — X
   END IF
END IF
```

Cascaded ELSE IF constructions can present the reader of the program with quite a problem – particularly when careful attention has not been paid to the layout and indentation of statements – in deciding which END IF belongs with which IF. For the programmer himself, the problem may be one of deciding whether he has remembered to close each IF with an END IF or, when the compiler indicates that an END IF may have been omitted, deciding where it ought to go. In the following examples, c1, c2 and c3 represent conditions and G1, G2 and G3 represent groups of statements to be executed if the respective conditions are true

```
IF (C1) THEN              IF (C1) THEN
  G1                        G1
ELSE                      ELSE IF (C2) THEN
  IF (C2) THEN              G2
    G2                    ELSE IF (C3) THEN
  ELSE                      G3
    IF (C3) THEN          ELSE
      G3                    G4
    ELSE                  END IF
      G4
    END IF
  END IF
END IF
```

Fig. 5.3 Fig. 5.4

The example of Fig. 5.4 illustrates the ELSE IF construction designed especially for the case of the cascaded IF after ELSE. Here, only a single END IF is needed to terminate all the IF alternatives.

Here is a more realistic piece of code: a variable called CODE is permitted to take only the values 0, 5 or 6, with a different action specified in each case.

```
IF (CODE .EQ. 0) THEN
  A = A + 1
ELSE IF (CODE .EQ. 5) THEN
  A = A + 2
ELSE IF (CODE .EQ. 6) THEN
  A = A + 3
ELSE
  PRINT *, 'CODE ', CODE, 'IS OUTSIDE',
*           ' THE PERMITTED RANGE'
END IF
```

## The logical IF

In the special case when there is only one statement to be executed if the given condition is true, and there is no alternative, the *logical* IF construction can be used.

The logical IF statement *never* has an ELSE clause, the THEN is *always* omitted, and the statement whose execution depends on the truth of the condition must appear immediately after the condition. This controlled statement is, literally, a single statement; it must not be another logical IF, block IF or DO (dealt with later) statement.

### Examples of the use of logical IF

```
(a)  IF (B**2 .GT. 4*A*C) PRINT *, 'REAL DISTINCT ROOTS'
(b)  DAYS = 365
     IF (LEAP) DAYS = 366
(c)  (alternative to (b))
     IF (.NOT. LEAP) DAYS = 365
     IF (LEAP)        DAYS = 366
```

Many programmers prefer (c) to (b), even though it is less 'efficient' in that it produces more machine language instructions and executes more of them at runtime – thus possibly slowing down the running program – because it is more explicit and does not involve a 'change of mind'.

(d) *(another possibility)*

```
         IF (LEAP) GO TO 90
         DAYS = 365
         GO TO 100
     90  DAYS = 366
    100  . . . etc.
```

This introduces another type of statement: the GO TO statement. Example (d) has two of these, neither of which has any *direct* connection with the original problem's solution. For this particular problem, solution (d) would generally be regarded as rather clumsy, (b) as the most efficient.

## The GO TO statement

This is a way of changing the sequence in which statements are executed, *unconditionally*. It is often called, for this reason, an *unconditional branch*. Its general form is

GO TO statement number

where 'statement number' is an integer in the range 1 to 99999. It means 'Take the next instruction from the statement labelled (in columns 1 to 5) with the given statement number and continue execution in sequence from that point'. Thus, GO TO 10 causes a branch to the statement labelled 10 and skips over any intervening statements without executing them.

The GO TO statement may be used for either forward or backward branches, but care is needed in using it for it can lead to programs that are difficult to understand. Generally speaking, each GO TO you use should be carefully examined to see if its use can be justified. Backward branches using the GO TO statement can be particularly confusing and are often replaceable by other constructions, as will be shown later.

Similarly, 'cascaded' GO TO statements, such as

```
      GO TO 10
      . . .
10    GO TO 15
      . . .
```

should be avoided: the first – if it is really needed – could be replaced by GO TO 15 directly.

Having said all that, it remains a fact that the controlled use of the GO TO statement is a very valuable feature of FORTRAN. Given a decision facility and an unconditional branch feature, we can now write programs involving *loops* – the repetition of selected groups of code completely automatically, with no need for the operator to intervene. This is one of the most powerful features of the computer and enables us to undertake much more realistic programming tasks.

The following program reads a value N, known only at runtime, and then a set of N values. It then calculates the average (mean) of those values and prints the result. Note the need, if the variable name MEAN is to be used for the average, to declare it as of REAL type. (Why?)

```
      PROGRAM AVRAGE
      REAL MEAN
```

```
C      READ IN THE NUMBER OF NUMBERS TO BE PROCESSED
       READ *, N
C      NOW CHECK THE VALIDITY OF N
       IF (N .LE. 0) THEN
        PRINT *, 'NO DATA.'
        GO TO 30
       END IF
C      WE NEED TO COUNT THE NUMBERS: KOUNT IS USED.
C      THEIR SUM IS ACCUMULATED IN THE VARIABLE SUM.
C      BOTH THESE NEED TO BE SET TO ZERO INITIALLY
       KOUNT = 0
       SUM   = 0.0
C      EACH TIME ROUND THE LOOP, WE CHECK TO SEE IF
C      ALL THE NUMBERS HAVE BEEN READ.
    10 IF (KOUNT .EQ. N) GO TO 20
C      IF NOT ...
       READ *, X
       SUM = SUM + X
C      INCREMENT THE COUNT
       KOUNT = KOUNT + 1
C      ... AND ROUND WE GO AGAIN
       GO TO 10
C      FINALLY, WE BRANCH TO HERE, WHERE WE
C      COMPUTE THE MEAN AND PRINT THE RESULT.
    20 MEAN = SUM/N
       PRINT *, 'MEAN OF ', N, ' VALUES IS ', MEAN
       PRINT *
C      THAT GIVES A BLANK LINE — FOR READABILITY
    30 PRINT *, 'END OF JOB'
C      THAT INDICATES TO YOU THAT THE PROGRAM
C      TERMINATED AT THE EXPECTED POINT.
       END
```

Note the use of comment lines in this example. One does not normally comment in quite so much detail as this, but *do* get into the habit of doing it *at the time you write your program*. You will never regret it.

One commonly sees, in the work of beginning (and often, alas, more experienced) programmers, sequences such as this:

```
       IF (A .EQ. B) GO TO 10
       GO TO 20
    10  ...
        ...      } sequence 1
       GO TO 30
    20  ...
        ...      } sequence 2
        ...
    30  ...
```

A very little thought shows that this contains an unnecessary GO TO statement as well as the correspondingly unwanted label. If one is constrained to use the logical IF (and the block IF was introduced to avoid this rather artificial way of doing things), a cleaner piece of code for the same problem would be the following:

```
      IF (A .NE. B) GO TO 20
      ...
      ...       } sequence 1
      ...
      GO TO 30
  20  ...
      ...
      ...       } sequence 2
      ...
  30  ...
```

Better still, use the block IF construction:

```
      IF (A .EQ. B) THEN
      ...
      ...       } sequence 1
      ...
      ELSE
      ...
      ...       } sequence 2
      ...
      END IF
```

Here we have no extraneous GO TO statements at all and no statement numbers to confuse matters.

## The computed GO TO statement

Consider this sequence, which might be used when writing a large program to select the section of that program to be executed next. The variable NEXT has been set to a value between 1 and 3 so that it can act as a selector. A value outside that range will cause a branch to statement number 4000; presumably some type of diagnostic action will be taken at that point in the program.

```
    IF (NEXT .EQ. 1) THEN
      GO TO 1000
    ELSE IF (NEXT .EQ. 2) THEN
      GO TO 2000
    ELSE IF (NEXT .EQ. 3) THEN
      GO TO 3000
    ELSE
      GO TO 4000
    END IF
```

This is tedious both to read and to write, especially if there are many labels from which to make the selection. An alternative way of coding it is this:

```
GO TO (1000, 2000, 3000), NEXT
GO TO 4000
```

which will have exactly the same effect. It is called the *computed* GO TO, and takes the general form

GO TO $(l1, l2, l3 \ldots ln), i$

where $l1, l2 \ldots ln$ are statement numbers; $i$ is an integer expression.

If $i = 1$, the statement behaves like GO TO $l1$; if $i = 2$, it behaves like GO TO $l2$, and so on. If $i$ is less than 1 or greater than $n$, the next statement in sequence is executed – in our example, this was GO TO 4000.

Some older versions of FORTRAN do not have this automatic fall-through to the next statement if the selector is out of range, and they may also insist that the selector be an integer variable – not an expression. In such a case, the example might be recoded as:

```
IF (NEXT .LT. 1 .OR. NEXT .GT. 3) GO TO 4000
GO TO (1000, 2000, 3000), NEXT
```

## Conclusion

Remember that computers will *execute* your programs, but *people* will read them. So make them readable to other people and, not least, yourself – you may have to amend this program a year or more from now! Choose meaningful names; use a pleasing layout; be consistent. I have tried, within the limits of modern typography, to lay out my examples as I hope you will.

Use GO TO if you must, but first try to ensure that there is no better alternative. There are some places you may *not* GO TO. At the moment, the most important of these is the block of statements between an IF and its corresponding END IF, from outside that block. It is also forbidden to branch between the various inner blocks of a block IF statement. A branch to the IF statement itself is permissible, but you may not branch to any line starting with an ELSE, ELSE IF or END IF. These restrictions are illustrated in Fig. 5.5.

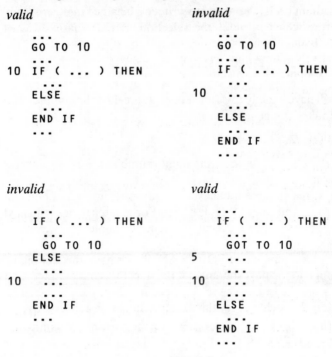

*valid*

```
    ...
    GO TO 10
    ...
10  IF ( ... ) THEN
    ...
    ELSE
    ...
    END IF
    ...
```

*invalid*

```
    ...
    GO TO 10
    ...
    IF ( ... ) THEN
      ...
10    ...
      ...
    ELSE
    ...
    END IF
    ...
```

*invalid*

```
    ...
    IF ( ... ) THEN
      ...
      GO TO 10
    ELSE
      ...
10    ...
      ...
    END IF
    ...
```

*valid*

```
    ...
    IF ( ... ) THEN
      ...
      GOT TO 10
5     ...
      ...
10    ...
      ...
    ELSE
    ...
    END IF
    ...
```

**Fig. 5.5**

## Exercises

1  For each of the following statements, say whether it is true or false.

   (a) The statement numbers indicate the order in which the statements of a FORTRAN program are to be obeyed.

   (b) The statement following a GO TO statement must have a statement number.

   (c) At most five statement numbers are permitted in a computed GO TO statement.

   (d) The following is a valid FORTRAN statement:

   ```
   GO TO (10, 20, 40, 30), J1
   ```

   (e) So is this:

   ```
   GO TO (40, 40, 50, 50) I+1
   ```

2 The variable KAJ can take only values between 454 and 457, inclusive. Branches to statements numbered 12, 13, 14 and 15 are to be made when the value of KAJ is 454, 455, 456, 457, respectively. Show how this may be achieved using:

    (a) a computed GO TO statement;

    (b) logical IF statements;

    (c) a block IF statement.

3 For each of the following, write the equivalent FORTRAN 77 condition.

    (a) DS is non-zero;

    (b) Q does not exceed zero, but T9 is zero;

    (c) A4 is not less than zero, or K has a value in the range 1 to 3, inclusive;

    (d) T is not equal to S, but the square of T is the same as the cube of V;

    (e) The value of C differs from those of D, E, F and G, or – if C is equal to F – D is less than the sum of E and G.

4 Write a complete FORTRAN 77 program that reads a sequence of positive values, checking that each one read is larger than its predecessor. The sequence ends with the value $-1$. If an out-of-sequence value is encountered before $-1$ is read, print 'SEQUENCE ERROR'. If $-1$ is reached without error, print 'VALID SEQUENCE'.

# 6

# Loops

Suppose we have just finished the week's shopping. Of course, we took a shopping list with us and, on this occasion, we wrote beside the name of each item on the list the quantity purchased and the price of each. So we might have something like this:

| Item | Quantity | Price (£) | Cost (£) | Running total (£) |
|------|----------|-----------|----------|-------------------|
| Butter | 4 | 0.53 | 2.12 | 2.12 |
| Cheese | 1½ | 1.04 | 1.56 | 3.68 |
| Cornflakes | 2 | 0.60 | 1.20 | 4.88 |
| Dog food | 7 | 0.29 | 2.03 | 6.91 |

So when we finish our shopping, we shall know what the bill at the checkout point will be.

This is a simple *loop* calculation; the same arithmetic process is being used many times over, but using different data each time. This is the process:

```
        Set the running total to zero.           ⎤
REPEAT  Get the next item;                       ⎥
        note its quantity and price;             ⎥  This is a
        calculate the cost (= quantity × price); ⎥  LOOP
        add the cost to the running total        ⎥
UNTIL   the last item has been dealt with.       ⎦
```

An alternative approach would have been to make a note of quantities and prices, with a view to checking the bill when we arrive home. If we have a computer at home, with a FORTRAN system, we could write a little program to do the sums. It might look like this:

```
    PROGRAM SHOPS
    TOTAL = 0.0
10  READ *, QTY, PRICE
    COST = QTY*PRICE
    TOTAL = TOTAL + COST
    PRINT *, QTY, PRICE, COST, TOTAL
    GO TO 10
    END
```

This is fine, most of the time, but in computing 'most of the time' is not enough. The programs we write have to work all the time. In this case there is the problem of termination; we have established the loop – 'GO TO 10' branching back to statement number 10 – but there is no way to leave it. The loop is endless. This is a rather unsatisfactory situation. The only way to stop the program is to switch off – a bit drastic – or have the operator or operating system invervene. In either case, you – the programmer – have allowed your program to run out of control. You should regard it as your responsibility *not* to let this happen. So we need some way of retaining control.

A test. for the end of data will suit this requirement, and the simplest way to achieve this, very often, is to introduce a *sentinel* value – a final value which is far outside the expected range of values that it may be taken as a signal that the last item has been read in. In our example, a ridiculous sentinel value, such as a 'quantity' of −1, would serve.

As the algorithm is presently specified, however, each time a set of values is read it is processed, and the test is made only after processing. It is obviously desirable that the sentinel value be detected *before* it is processed as though it were valid data! A rearrangement of the algorithm would enable this to be achieved. For instance:

> Set the running total to zero.
> Read the next item's quantity and price.
> REPEAT  Calculate the cost (= quantity × price);
>             add the cost to the running total;
>             read the next item's quantity and price
> UNTIL   a quantity of −1 is read.

We can code this in FORTRAN as follows:

```
    TOTAL = 0.0
    READ *, QTY, PRICE
10  COST = QTY*PRICE
    TOTAL = TOTAL + COST
    PRINT *, QTY, PRICE, COST, TOTAL
    READ *, QTY, PRICE
    IF (QTY.GT.-1) GO TO 10
    END
```

This time, when a quantity (QTY) of −1 is read – together with a
PRICE value, which will be ignored – the loop back to statement
number 10 will not be executed, and a controlled exit is made.

A problem with this approach is that you need to be absolutely
sure that there is at least one 'real' item to be processed. If, for some
reason, the first data item read were to have −1 as its quantity, the
calculation would be performed on meaningless data (−1 packets of
butter) and an attempt would be made to read more data after the
'result' had been printed. Almost anything could happen at this
point, because there is probably no more data! Once again, the
programmer has lost control.

What can we do? Well, how about testing at the *top* of the loop,
instead of the bottom? That way, if we read the sentinel as part of
the first item, we can branch around the loop and ignore it
completely. The pseudocode would look like this:

> Set the running total to zero.
> Read the first quantity.
> WHILE the quantity exceeds −1,
>> read the price;
>> calculate the cost (= quantity × price);
>> add the cost to the running total;
>> print quantity, price, cost and total;
>> read the next quantity.

You will notice that there have been some slight adjustments. The
quantity and price are now read separately, so there is no need for a
superfluous price value to be input at the end. I have also included
the output operation in the pseudocode to complete the algorithm,
which translates quite easily into FORTRAN as follows:

```
    TOTAL = 0.0
    READ *, QTY
```

```
10  IF (QTY.GT.-1) THEN
      READ *, PRICE
      COST = QTY*PRICE
      TOTAL = TOTAL + COST
      PRINT *, QTY, PRICE, COST, TOTAL
      READ *, QTY
      GO TO 10
    END IF
    END
```

This is what, in today's terms, is called a well-structured loop. It has only one entry point and one exit point. The whole thing may be regarded as a 'black box' that performs a specific task – printing and totalling the shopping list. Unfortunately, the names of the items are not included; we shall see later how this can be achieved.

## 'Counting' loops

In the case of the shopping list, we had to find a way of signalling 'end of data', because we did not know – until we reached the end of the list – how many items it contained. Very often, in practice, we know either exactly how many loops will be required or the name of a variable in which the number of loops is held. For example, we may wish to read in 100 values and determine their average. We could do it like this:

```
    SUM = 0.0
    KOUNT = 0
10  IF (KOUNT.LT.100) THEN
      READ *, X
      SUM = SUM + X
      KOUNT = KOUNT + 1
      GO TO 10
    END IF
    AVRAGE = SUM/100
```

Initially, the count of the number of values read (KOUNT) is set to zero; the SUM of those values (each value represented by x), since none has yet been read, is also set to zero. (Incidentally, why KOUNT, rather than COUNT? And why AVRAGE, rather then AVERAGE?) Each time a value is read, as long as KOUNT is less than 100, that value is added to the SUM, the KOUNT is increased by 1, and GO TO 10 causes a branch back to the IF statement. Eventually, when the 100th value has been added in, the test will fail (since KOUNT will then be 100), and the statement following END IF will be executed. Here, the average is calculated, and the loop has been left.

## The DO loop

There is no reason why, if you want to, you should not set up all your loops in the ways demonstrated so far. Yet there is another approach that is usually more efficient in the way that it makes use of the computer's internal resources. It is called the DO loop. To illustrate its use, the same averaging algorithm has been recoded using a DO loop:

```
    SUM = 0.0
    DO 10 KOUNT = 1, 100, 1
      READ *, X
      SUM = SUM + X
10  CONTINUE
    AVRAGE = SUM/100
    ... etc.
```

The advantages of using the DO loop are three-fold:

1 The loop is more compact.
2 It usually produces more efficient machine code.
3 You do not have to bother about looking after the loop-control variable – KOUNT, in this example – since it is done automatically.

The DO loop is one of the most useful features of FORTRAN; let us take a closer look at it. First, we shall see how a DO loop is set up.

The group of statements that will constitute the body of the loop – that is, those statements that are to be repeated – have first to be determined. In the example, these are:

```
READ *, X
SUM = SUM + X
```

We place after the last statement of this group a CONTINUE statement, preceded by an unused statement number. (The use of CONTINUE, though not strictly necessary, is strongly recommended. It is the safest way to terminate a DO loop. If you do not use CONTINUE, the rules become quite complicated because, basically, the terminating statement of a DO loop can be any executable statement *except* one that would cause a branch out of the loop. This includes GO TO, DO, the block IF and several others; a logical IF may be all right if the controlled statement is not a species of branch. For full details see the FORTRAN 77 standard or your system reference manual. For the time being, stick to CONTINUE.)

In the example we used the statement number 10. We now have the body of the loop and its terminating statement, constituting the *range* of the loop:

```
      READ *, X
      SUM = SUM + X
10 CONTINUE
```

Next we put the DO statement at the head of the loop:

```
   DO 10 KOUNT = 1,100,1
```

which we interpret as 'DO all the statements in the range of the loop (i.e. down to and including the one labelled 10) as long as the value of KOUNT does not exceed 100. Initially, KOUNT is to be set to a value of 1 and each time around the loop that value is to be increased by 1. When KOUNT exceeds 100, go to the statement immediately after that labelled 10.'

There are four numbers in this DO statement. The first is always a statement number, and identifies the last statement in the range of the DO loop; the numbers after the '=' represent, in order, the initial value and limit value of the loop control (or DO) variable – KOUNT in this case – and the amount by which the value of that variable is to be changed each time through the loop (the 'increment'). Note the punctuation; it is quite important. If you prefer, you may add one extra comma after the statement number:

```
   DO 10, KOUNT = 1,100,1
```

If the increment is 1, as it often is, it may be omitted, together with its preceding comma:

```
   DO 10 KOUNT = 1,100    or    DO 10, KOUNT = 1,100
```

## How many loops?

In practice, it is not necessary to know the values of all the DO parameters (initial value, limit and increment) at the time the program is written. Any or all of them can be arithmetic expressions, and the simplest arithmetic expression, apart from a number, is a variable name. So we can have DO statements such as this:

```
DO 25 K = 1,N
```

in which the statements in the range of the DO will be executed N times, the value of N being determined at the time the program is run. For example, the fragment that follows reads a value NUM, followed by that many pairs of values representing $(x,y)$ coordinates. As each pair is read in, its distance from the coordinate origin $(0,0)$ is calculated, using the formula

$$d = \sqrt{x^2 + y^2}$$

```
      ...
      READ *, NUM
      DO 25 I = 1, NUM
        READ *, X, Y
        D = SQRT(X*X + Y*Y)
        PRINT *, X, Y, D
25    CONTINUE
      ... etc.
```

Nor need the increment always be 1. If we were calculating the prime numbers greater than 2, we should only be interested in the odd values, since all the even ones are divisible by 2. If all possible values up to 1000 were to be considered, we could control the loop with a statement such as:

DO 19 K = 3,999,2

'Start with K = 3, finish with K = 999 and increase K by 2 on each loop.' Only the odd values between and including these limits will now be used. The actual *number* of loops performed is calculated before the first 'trip' through the loop, and so it is called the *trip count*. It is calculated using the formula:

$$\text{trip count} = \left\lfloor \frac{\text{limit} - \text{initial value}}{\text{increment}} \right\rfloor + 1$$

where $\left\lfloor \ldots \right\rfloor$ means 'the largest whole number not exceeding . . . .'

If the trip count is negative or zero, the statements in the range of the DO are not executed at all.

**Examples**

| *DO statement* | *Trip count* | |
|---|---|---|
| DO 10 I = 1,100 | 100 | |
| DO 10 I = 3,999,2 | 499 | |
| DO 10 I = −1,−100,−1 | 100 | |
| DO 10 I = 20,−20,−2 | 21 | |
| DO 10 I = 1,10,−1 | −8 | (loop is ignored, trip count is effectively 0) |
| DO 10 I = 3,20,5 | 4 | ($I$ = 3, 8, 13, 18) |
| DO 10 X = −0.5,1.5,0.1 | 21 | |

In general, it is best to avoid loops such as that of the last example, in which the DO parameters have real (i.e. non-integer) values. Remember that the 'real' values in a computer are usually only close approximations to the true mathematical values and, like all approximations, contain a slight but none the less real error. This does not often cause problems, but we need to be aware of it and on the look out for situations in which trouble can arise. One of those situations is that in which a large number of such values are added, because each addition can and does introduce error to the extent that the final value calculated may differ quite appreciably from the true result. This can mean that when we have real loop parameters, as here, the final test of the value of the DO variable against the limit may fail, because of the errors introduced in adding the increment so many times. In consequence, the loop may be executed too few or too many times. It is better to use integer loop parameters whenever possible – which, in practice, is always. Earlier versions of FORTRAN would not allow anything but integer loop parameters, and many experienced programmers feel that the relaxation of this rule in FORTRAN 77 is a retrograde step.

In this case, a simple transformation can be used while retaining the accuracy of the count:

```
DO 10 IX = −5,15,1
X = IX/10.0
```

An integer DO variable has been introduced, IX, and this is divided by 10 to give the real value x needed in the loop body. A better way to write the DO statement now would be

```
DO 10 IX = −5,15
```

since the increment is 1.

## Loops in loops

It is quite common to have loops that include other loops. We shall see a number of examples of this later, when we consider arrays, but the point is illustrated by the following example in which five sets of data are read in, each data set consisting of 10 pairs of values – weights expressed as pounds and ounces. Within each data set, the total weight is accumulated and printed in both ounces and kilogrammes.

```
      PROGRAM METRIC
      INTEGER TOTAL, COUNT, WEIGHT, POUNDS, OUNCES
      REAL    KILOS
C
C        SET UP THE OUTER COUNT: FIVE SETS OF DATA'
C
      DO 20 COUNT = 1,5
         TOTAL = 0
C
C        SET UP THE INNER COUNT:
C        10 ITEMS IN EACH DATA SET
      DO 15 WEIGHT = 1,10
         READ *, POUNDS, OUNCES
         TOTAL = 16*POUNDS + OUNCES + TOTAL
   15 CONTINUE
C
C        CONVERT TO METRIC AND PRINT
C
      KILOS = TOTAL/35.274
      PRINT *, 'DATA SET: ',COUNT, TOTAL, ' OZ = ',
     *          KILOS, ' KG'
   20 CONTINUE
      END
```

When one loop is inside another one, like this, it is said to be *nested*. Remember that the innermost nested loop will be entered last and will complete its execution first. The more deeply a loop is nested, the more times its statements will be executed. One should always try to write efficient code, but particular care should be taken when writing inner loops. There is no formal limit on the depth to which loops may be nested, but a physical limit may be set by the computer being used. Consult your reference manual to see if there is a restriction for the machine you normally use. Typically, such restrictions specify a maximum nesting depth of, for example, 16 or 32 – 16 or 32 loops, one inside the other. This is no restriction at all, in practice, since loops more than five deep are rarely encountered.

Nesting must be proper in the sense that nested loops must be completely contained one within the other; overlapping is not permitted. Valid and invalid nestings are illustrated in Fig. 6.1.

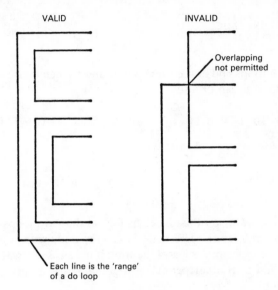

**Fig. 6.1**

It follows that the following code represents an invalid construction:

```
    DO 40 I = 1,24
      READ *, N
      DO 50 J = 1,N
        READ *, A
        S = S+A
40  CONTINUE
50    CONTINUE
```

In any case, the construction is not very meaningful. It is likely to have arisen by accident.

DO loops can occur within *either* the THEN *or* the ELSE part of a block IF, but a loop may not extend from the THEN part into the ELSE part.

Quite often, two or more loops will logically terminate at the same point:

```
      ...
      DO 20 I = 1,20
      ...
         DO 10 J = 1,30
         ...
         ...
10       CONTINUE
20    CONTINUE
      ...
```

Here, both loops end at the same point, and in such a case a single loop terminator can be used:

```
      ...
      DO 10 I = 1,20
      ...
         DO 10 J = 1,30
         ...
         ...
10    CONTINUE                 – common terminator
      ...
```

Personally, I never do this; it seems logical that two loops should have two terminators. The code is clearer and, with a modern compiler, no efficiency is lost. I mention it because you will almost certainly find it in other people's programs – it is a very popular construction.

A DO loop may *only* be entered through its initial DO statement. A branch into the middle of a DO loop from outside the range of that DO is illegal. However, it is permissible to branch *out* of a DO loop at any point, either backwards or forwards. When this happens, the value of the DO variable after the branch has been performed is the last value it was given before the exit from the loop.

When a DO loop terminates normally, the value of the DO variable will be one increment beyond the limit, that is, where the trip count is $N$,

inititial value $+ N \times$ increment

The value of the DO variable is available for use inside the loop, but it is not permissible to change it.

Finally, it *is* permissible to change the values of variables used to specify the initial value, limit or increment, but any such change will have no effect on the trip count once the DO statement has been executed.

## The STOP statement

The effect of this statement is to terminate the program currently executing but, unlike the END statement, it may appear anywhere in the executable part of the program. It has the general form:

STOP

or, possibly,

STOP *n*

where *n* is a string of up to five digits or a CHARACTER constant. This value is displayed when the stop occurs and enables one to determine exactly which STOP statement (if there are several) has been obeyed.

## The PAUSE statement

This consists of the single word

PAUSE

or

PAUSE *n*

in which *n* takes the same form as in the STOP statement.

This causes the program to halt temporarily so that, for instance, the operator or user can take some essential action, such as mounting a magnetic tape or disc containing required data on a suitable device, or putting special preprinted paper into the printer. When this has been done, the operator – or sometimes the user, if he is working at a terminal – can issue a command from his console that will restart the program at the statement immediately following that which caused the pause.

A suitable use might be the following:

```
. . .
PAUSE 'PLEASE CHANGE PAPER IN PRINTER 1'
. . .
```

## Exercises

1 How many times are the loops controlled by the following DO
   statements executed?
   (a)   DO 10 I = 1, 10
   (b)   DO 10 I = 1, 10, 2
   (c)   DO 10 I = 1, 100, 25
   (d)   DO 10 I = −5, 20, 3
   (e)   DO 10 I = 20, −5, 4
   (f)   DO 10 I = −5, −10, −2
   (g)   DO 10 I = 12, −4, −4
2 Write a program that will read in 30 values of $x$ and the
   corresponding values of $y$, and calculate and print a table of $x$, $y$
   and the square root of $(x^2 + y^2)$.
3 Data consists of groups of integer values, the first value in each
   group being the number of values in the rest of the group. There
   are five such groups. Write a program that will read the groups
   and calculate and print (a) the mean of each group and (b) the
   overall mean. A suitable set of data for testing might be 1,1,
   2,1,2, 3,1,2,3, 4,1,2,3,4, 5,1,2,3,4,5 which gives group means
   of 1.0, 1.5, 2.0, 2.5 and 3.0, and an overall mean of 2.3333.

# 7

# Arrays

Let us have another look at the shopping list with which we started the last chapter. Suppose we have collected together all the information about each item in the list – name (or stock number), quantity and price – and we want to compute and print the cost of each item. The *list* is an important idea in data processing, since it usually denotes a set of similar items that we can treat in much the same way. When this is possible, we can often organise our program around a loop and thus reduce its size and complexity. *Tables* of data are similarly important, and the term *array* is used to denote both types of data structure. Our shopping list can be considered as consisting of three simpler lists: a list of items, a corresponding list of quantities and another of prices. Each of these three sublists an important feature of arrays in general: each has entries all of the same type – item names, or codes, for the first, real numbers for the other two. An array is an indexed collection of data items, all of the same type.

The operations we want to perform on the entries in our shopping list are quite simple, but the list could be very long indeed. It would be very inconvenient if we had to give a different variable name to each item, quantity and price. We could do so, of course, using names such as ITEM1, ITEM2, ITEM3, systematically changing the name for each new item. In the same way, the quantity and price for ITEM1 could be named QTY1 and PRICE1; those for ITEM2 could be QTY2 and PRICE2; and so on. Fig. 7.1 is part of a flowchart showing the processing when such a naming scheme is used.

This is not at all satisfactory. A set of what is essentially the same

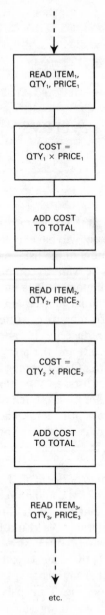

**Fig. 7.1**

instructions has to be written for each entry in the list. This implies that we shall need a different program if we change our list, because if the number of entries is changed, so is the number of instructions. It would be much better if we could write a general set of instructions applicable to any item and arrange to repeat them for each item until the list was exhausted. What we need is a loop, but with automatic progression from one list entry to the next each time around. We shall achieve this by treating our list as an array and using *subscripted variables*. In fact, as you will see, we shall use three arrays.

Consider first the items on the list. What we shall do is use *one* variable name for identifying information – item name or stock code – of *all* items. It seems reasonable to choose the name (or *identifier*) ITEM. On the face of it, this does not help much; there may be many items, but we have only one name – a possibly confusing situation. Ah, but we shall distinguish the various items from one another by qualifying the name, using a *subscript*: the first item can be referred to as $ITEM_1$, the second as $ITEM_2$, etc. Now the word ITEM is the name of an array of values, each *element* of the array being the name (or stock code) of a different item. We distinguish one element from another by its subscript, which is the relative position of that element in the array. Fig. 7.2 illustrates this idea, using a unique code (the stock code) to identify the type of item. For example, '221' may mean 'butter', '415' may be the code for 'dog food'. We shall see in Chapter 8 how strings of characters may be stored in arrays.

In the same way, we can organise arrays for the quantity and price of each item, in such a way that $QTY_i$ and $PRICE_i$ represent, respectively, the quantity and price of $ITEM_i$. It follows that we can compute the cost of $ITEM_i$ as $QTY_i{}^*PRICE_i$.

Notice that ITEM is implicitly the name of an integer variable, so

The array 'ITEM'

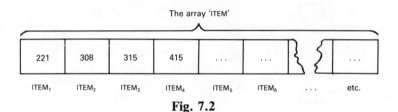

Fig. 7.2

all the elements of the array ITEM must be integers, unless we choose to write an overriding type declaration at the head of the program. Similarly, QTY and PRICE are arrays of real values.

It is not possible, with the sort of equipment usually available, to type subscripts in the way shown above when preparing a program for input to a computer. In practice, we have to write, for instance, $ITEM_3$ as ITEM(3), with the subscript in parentheses following the variable name. The parentheses are very important and must not be omitted. This does not, as you might think, break the rule about special characters not being allowed in variable names: the name here is ITEM, and (3) is the subscript held in parentheses. ITEM(3) is a *subscripted variable*. The subscript must *always* be of *integer* type, but it may take the form of an integer constant, an integer variable, or an arithmetic expression producing an integer value.

For example, we could write QTY(J), and the particular element of the array QTY to which we refer would depend on the current value of the integer variable J. If J has the value of 5, we shall be considering the element $QTY_5$. We could change the value of J to 29, in which case we should be dealing with $QTY_{29}$, and so on. Instead of having to rename the variables when we refer to a different item and write the instructions again, all that is now needed is to arrange to change the value of J after each calculation and then use the same instructions over again. Fig. 7.3 is a flowchart for the shopping list problem, using this principle, and here is an equivalent FORTRAN 77 program, though it is not quite complete.

```
      . . .
C        READ IN THE ITEM, QUANTIFY AND PRICE ARRAYS,
C        TERMINATED BY AN ITEM VALUE OF 0, OR LESS
      KOUNT = 0
      READ *, I
   10 IF (I.GT.0) THEN
         KOUNT = KOUNT + 1
         ITEM(KOUNT) = I
         READ *, QTY(KOUNT), PRICE(KOUNT)
         READ *, I
         GO TO 10
      END IF
C        THE DATA IS NOW ALL IN, AND KOUNT WILL
C        CONTAIN THE NUMBER OF ITEMS READ
      TOTAL = 0.0
      DO 20 K = 1,KOUNT
         COST = QTY(K)*PRICE(K)
         TOTAL = TOTAL + COST
```

```
      PRINT *, ITEM(K), QTY(K), PRICE(K), COST
20 CONTINUE
    PRINT *, 'TOTAL COST IS: ', TOTAL
    ...
    END
```

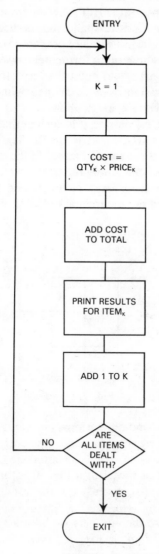

**Fig. 7.3**

The subscripting facility is one of the most useful features of high-level language such as FORTRAN, but it can be applied more broadly than we have seen so far. Up until now we have considered only the 'one-dimensional' array – that is, the element is selected by using a single subscript. But FORTRAN does not restrict us to the one-dimensional case, and we shall often find two or even three subscripts useful. In fact, the standard permits us to have as many as seven subscripts though, perhaps fortunately, opportunities for the use of such complex arrays do not arise very often.

What are the circumstances in which one might want to use more than one subscript? Here is an example.

The diagram (Fig. 7.4) shows a grid such as that used for playing the game of Noughts and Crosses (or Tic-Tac-Toe). It contains nine squares, arranged in three rows of three. In the diagram, the rows and the columns have been numbered from 1 to 3. Suppose each of the squares represents an array element, and it is required to determine the value in the square marked 'x'. Let us call the whole array SQUARE.

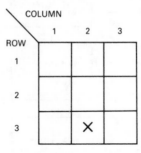

**Fig. 7.4**

Now, if SQUARE is a one-dimensional array it is not at all obvious from the picture how we should refer to element x. If the data items are stored a row at a time, x will be SQUARE(8), because it is the last-but-one on the last row. But if they are stored a column at a time, x will be SQUARE(6), because it is the last entry in the second column.

If, however, we use the numbers we have associated with each row and column (row number first), it is possible to be quite precise as to which array element is labelled 'x'. It is the one in row 3, column 2. We can abbreviate this to a pair of subscripts (3, 2). So we declare SQUARE to be a two-dimensional array (i.e. it has breadth as well as length) and refer to the square 'x' as SQUARE(3, 2) because it is at the intersection of the 3rd row and the 2nd column. Note the comma separating the subscripts; it must never be omitted. Without that comma, it would appear to the compiler as though we were talking about the 32nd element of a one-dimensional array.

You may leave as many spaces as you like between the name of the array and the left parenthesis preceding the subscripts. Spaces are used in FORTRAN primarily as a means of improving the readability of the program and, with one exception – dealt with later, and easily remembered – are ignored by the compiler. So use them freely. The following ways of referring to the centre element of SQUARE are all equivalent:

```
SQUARE(2,2)    SQUARE( 2, 2 )
SQUARE(2,2)    S Q U A R E ( 2 , 2 )
SQUARE (2, 2) SQU AR E ( 2 , 2)
```

We could have reorganised the shopping list data structure in terms of a two-dimensional array, though I should be disinclined to do so in view of the loss of clarity in the code. Fig. 7.5 illustrates the structure. Note, however, that doing it this way means, since all the elements of an array have to be of the same type, that we shall have to choose either to use real numbers for the items' stock codes – not

|   | 1          | 2        | 3     |
|---|------------|----------|-------|
|   | Stock code | Quantity | Price |
| 1 | 221        | 4        | 53    |
| 2 | 308        | 2        | 104   |
| 3 | 315        | 2        | 60    |
| 4 | 415        | 7        | 29    |
| 5 | . . .      | . . .    | . . . |

**Fig. 7.5**

really a very good idea – or express both quantity and price as integers. So far as price is concerned, this is probably the best approach, because there is no possibility of the rounding errors to which real values are prone affecting the stock values. It may, however, be a problem if fractional quantities are common.

Assuming, nevertheless, that the structure of Fig. 7.5 is adopted, with integer values, the key statements of the program now become:

```
INTEGER STOCK, TOTAL, COST
...
...
STOCK(KOUNT, 1) = I
READ *, STOCK(KOUNT, 2), STOCK(KOUNT, 3)
...
...
  COST = STOCK(KOUNT, 2) * STOCK(KOUNT, 3)
  ...
  PRINT *, STOCK(KOUNT, 1), STOCK(KOUNT, 2),
*          STOCK(KOUNT, 3), COST
```

It has now lost much of its readability.

## Array declaration

Before a computer can process data, it must have somewhere to hold it. This place is the computer's memory, or store. The memory may be considered as being subdivided into *memory cells* (or *store locations*), each of which can hold one item of data – usually a number.

It is no good storing data away in memory if you cannot retrieve it when you need to use it, so we need to be able to identify every individual memory cell. This is done by having a *memory address* associated permanently with each cell, rather like the number on each house in a street. When you see Joe Bloggs go into number 42, you know that you can then go to that house with confidence that you will find him. In the same way, if you put the value 3.14159 into memory cell 41563, you may have every confidence that – as long as you do not put something else into the same cell in the meantime – when you ask for the contents of cell 41563, you will receive the value 3.14159. One of the joys of using a language like FORTRAN is that you do not have to remember these nasty memory addresses – the compiler does that for you. You simply choose names for your variables (the correct term is *identifiers*) and the compiler's job is to ensure that each identifier has a memory cell (for a simple variable) or a group of memory cells (for an array) reserved for it, and that any reference to that identifier will always result in an internal reference to the reserved memory cells.

With simple variables, such as x, ALPHA or PI, there is no problem. A memory cell is reserved for each variable as it is encountered for the first time during compilation. For subscripted variables, however, a little more care is needed. Suppose we have a subscripted variable called LIST, a two-dimensional array with four rows and three columns. How will the compiler know how many memory cells to reserve for LIST?

We know that it needs $4 \times 3$, i.e. 12 memory cells. How do we tell the compiler? It is usually done by means of the DIMENSION statement, thus:

```
DIMENSION LIST(1:4, 1:3)
```

Similarly, a one-dimensional array called STRING, having 30 elements could be declared by:

```
DIMENSION STRING(1:30)
```

Both declarations might be combined into one, like this:

```
DIMENSION LIST(1:4, 1:3), STRING(1:30)
```

In the parentheses following the array name are as many pairs of values as the array has subscripts. The two values of each pair are separated by a colon, and are called, respectively, the lower and upper bounds of the subscript. In our example, the first subscript of LIST is declared to have a minimum value of 1 and a maximum value of 4. This is a great help to the compiler in generating code that can check for violation of these limits when the program is running. In the same way, it should now be apparent that the subscript bounds of STRING are from 1 to 30. With this information, it is straightforward for the compiler to work out how much memory space the array will need. The lower bound *must* be less than the upper bound, but it need not be '1'. Mathematicians often number their array elements starting from zero:

```
DIMENSION X(0:99)
```

declares a 100-element array $x_0 \, x_1 \, x_2 \, x_3 \, \ldots \, x_{98} \, x_{99}$. There is no restriction on the upper bounds of an array, though there may be physical restriction set by the size of memory.

As shown in the following example, each array declared must have its own set of bounds, even if this is the same for several arrays:

```
DIMENSION ITEM(1:100), QTY(1:100), PRICE(1:100)
```

However, in the very common event that the lower bound is 1, it may be omitted:

```
DIMENSION A(100), Q(20,30), X(0:99)
```

Note that x's bounds have to be given in full, since the lower bound is *not* 1.

In this last example, if any of the arrays shown were of another type, it would be sufficient to add the appropriate type declaration:

```
INTEGER Q
DIMENSION A(100), Q(20,30), X(0:99)
```

Alternatively, the array declaration can be combined with the type declaration. This may result in there being no need for the DIMENSION statement:

```
INTEGER Q(20,30)
DIMENSION A(100), X(0:99)
```

As we shall see later, an array may also be dimensioned using a COMMON statement. However it is done, the dimension information must not appear in the program unit more than once, and the declaration must precede any attempt to make use of the array or any of its elements.

We can now see that the incompleteness of the shopping list example is a result of an omitted array declaration. The first line should be

```
DIMENSION ITEM(100), QTY(100), PRICE(100)
```

and could be followed by

```
C      ALLOWS FOR A LIST OF AT MOST 100 ITEMS
```

## Exercises

1 Refer to Fig. 7.5 and write down the subscripts of the following array elements:

(a) The stock code of the item whose price is 29;

(b) The quantity of the item whose stock code is 308;

(c) The price of the item of which there are 4 in stock.

What are the values of the following elements of the same array? (Use ITEMS as the name of the array.)

(d) ITEMS(1, 2)   (e) ITEMS(3, 3)   (f) ITEMS(2, 1)

2 A is a 6 × 17 array, and both subscripts have a lower bound of 1. GIN is a 3 × 4 array, whose subscripts have lower bounds of 0. D has only three elements, and is one-dimensional. DATE is a 10 × 52 × 3 array. Both D and DATE have subscripts with a lower bound of 1. Write *one* suitable DIMENSION statement.

3 Can you spot the errors?

(a)   DIMENSON C(30)

(b)   DIMENSION A(2, 2), B(7) N(16)

4 MAT is a 10 × 10 integer array. Write a FORTRAN statement sequence to transpose it into the new array MATE, squaring each term in the process. When a matrix is transposed, the rows are written as columns, and vice versa. For example (3 × 3 arrays are used here, to save space)

```
if MAT is  1  2  3                    1 16 49
           4  5  6 the result will be: 4 25 64
           7  8  9                    9 36 81
```

5 Write a complete program that reads in 100 values, a row at a time, to the 10 × 10 array SQUARE. Each element may only have the value 0 or 1. When all the data has been input, the program should then read in pairs of values, (I, J), representing row number and column number, and print the number of '0' values in the squares immediately surrounding the specified square. Repeat this until a negative I-value is read. Simple data checks should be included in the program.

# 8

# Adding a little character

This section introduces the statements and operations needed to enable your programs to manipulate alphabetic, numeric, punctuation and other characters as well as text items composed of these characters.

## Character-valued data

Just as we are able to handle problems involving numbers, using real and integer constants and variables, it is often useful to be able to deal with non-numeric data in the same way. For instance, we might want to sort a list of names into alphabetical order; or to reorganise a page of text so that the right-hand margin is straightened out; or scan a list and extract all the entries relating to the name SMITH; or count the number of occurrences of the word 'honourable' in a parliamentary speech. All these problems have a common feature: they involve operations on a string of characters – textual manipulation. It is very useful to be able to define data as being of the type CHARACTER and to have a set of operations available that will enable us to handle such data. FORTRAN 77 gives us this capability.

We have already seen in passing one or two examples of character *constants*. For example, in Chapter 7 the statement

```
PRINT *, 'TOTAL COST IS: ', TOTAL
```

appeared, the effect of which is to print the character string TOTAL COST IS: followed by the value of the variable TOTAL. The string of characters enclosed in single quotation marks is a character constant. An interesting question that arises almost at once is: 'If the constant is enclosed inside quotation marks, how is a quotation mark represented? The answer is that two consecutive quote marks are taken to mean that a single quote is to appear at that point. So 'WATCH O''ER HIM' will print as WATCH O'ER HIM.

Incidentally, take care not to confuse these two single quotes with the double-quote character available on many keyboards. They are *not* synonymous, and the required effect will not be obtained.

In dealing with numbers, we saw how useful it was to hold numeric values in named variables; character strings can be held in exactly the same way in *character variables*. Such variables must be declared at the head of the program unit in which they are used, by means of the CHARACTER type declaration. This gives the compiler two essential pieces of information: the *name* of the variable and the *length* of the character string it can hold. From this information, the amount of memory that must be reserved for the variable can be determined at compile time.

```
CHARACTER * 10 NAME1, NAME2
```

declares two variables – NAME1 and NAME2 – each capable of holding a string of 10 characters. If character variables of different lengths are needed, they can be declared by using several CHARACTER declarations:

```
CHARACTER * 4 A, B
CHARACTER * 5 C, D
CHARACTER * 7 E
```

Here, A and B are declared as character variables of length 4, C and D are 5-character variables, and E is 7 characters in length.

This is probably the clearest method of declaring a number of character variables of different lengths, but there is another way of associating length with name:

```
CHARACTER * 4 A, B, C * 5, D * 5, E * 7
```

achieves the same result in a single statement. Here, 'C * 5' ensures that the length of C is five characters, not four; in the same way, D will be of length five, and E of length seven characters.

When a length is attached to a name by an asterisk, it takes precedence over that following the word 'CHARACTER', which may be regarded as a default value, to be used only if no other is specified. Thus, A and B are four characters in length because no alternative is given. Had we written:

```
CHARACTER * 4 A, B, C, D * 5, E * 7
```

then C would have been allocated the default length of four characters. If no length is specified after the word 'CHARACTER', a default value of one is assumed:

```
CHARACTER FIRST, NEXT, LAST * 15
```

specifies that FIRST and NEXT are single-character variables, but LAST can hold 15 characters.

Obviously, the length attribute must have an integer value – you cannot sensibly have a string of, for example, 4.875 characters – but the value given may be in the form of an expression if that seems a reasonable way to do it. This may well be the case if, for instance, the most convenient number of characters to be stored in a variable is dependent on the particular computer being used. Something like this:

```
CHARACTER * (3 + 4 * 2) ITEM
```

is not, in general, very useful – we could just as well have written

```
CHARACTER * 11 ITEM
```

But FORTRAN 77 gives us the option of naming our constants, you will recall, by using the PARAMETER statement. Several constants may be named in a single PARAMETER statement, which should appear at the head of the program unit before any reference to the defined identifiers:

```
INTEGER P
PARAMETER (K = 10, N = 5, P = 3 * N)
```

Note that P, which is implicitly the name of a REAL quantity, is specified as of type INTEGER *before* it is given a value in the PARAMETER statement. You will no doubt have noticed that, once the value of N has been given, its name can be used in the subsequent expression for P. Such an expression is called a *constant expression*, since it consists solely of constant values and constant names, together with arithmetic operators.

The length attribute of a character variable can be specified by a constant expression, so something like this:

```
PARAMETER (N = 4)
CHARACTER * (2 * N + 1) ITEM
```

is quite valid. It is worth noting that there may be many references in the program to N, and that changing just the one PARAMETER statement will effectively change all those references. This would certainly not be the case if we had used the value 4 instead of the name N.

There is no reason why a named constant should not be a character string, but in such a case the name needs to be declared as of type CHARACTER *before* the PARAMETER statement:

```
CHARACTER * 6 CAPTAL
PARAMETER (CAPTAL = 'LISBON')
```

Here we have declared CAPTAL to be a six-character value, and assigned to it the constant LISBON. If we were now to execute.

```
PRINT *, CAPTAL
```

the output would be

```
LISBON
```

## Character arrays

There is no problem in defining an array of character strings. It may be done either by using a DIMENSION statement or in the CHARACTER type declaration:

```
CHARACTER * 15 SHIP
DIMENSION SHIP(50)
```

or

```
CHARACTER * 15 SHIP(50)
```

or, less elegantly, perhaps,

```
CHARACTER SHIP(50) * 15
```

Values may be assigned to such variables by reading them from some input device:

```
      DO 10 I = 1,50
        READ *, SHIP(I)
   10 CONTINUE
```

If this method is adopted, each data item must be enclosed in single quotes (we shall see later that there are somewhat less clumsy alternatives), thus:

'FEARLESS' 'INVINCIBLE' 'BRITANNIA' . . . etc.

When, as in these cases, the data item is smaller than the available space in the character variable, it is stored at the extreme left and padded out with spaces. We should thus have, from the above data,

```
SHIP(1)    FEARLESS_____
SHIP(2)    INVINCIBLE_____
SHIP(3)    BRITANNIA_____
```

(in each case, the spaces are indicated by an underline _). We can also use the normal assignment statement:

```
SHIP(4) = 'UGANDA'
SHIP(5) = 'CANBERRA'
SHIP(6) = 'PRIDE_OF_GRIMSBY'
```

In this last example, though, we seem to have slipped up a little. 'PRIDE_OF_GRIMSBY' is a 16-character name – including the spaces, which are, of course, characters, even though we cannot see them when they are 'printed'. Such a case results in the excess characters' being simply chopped off, and we shall finish up with

```
SHIP(4)    UGANDA_____
SHIP(5)    CANBERRA_____
SHIP(6)    PRIDE_OF_GRIMSB
```

This is rather unfortunate, but we should have been more careful at the planning stage. Changing the declaration to

```
CHARACTER * 20 SHIP(50)
```

would cure the immediate fault, but we should check through the list of names to see what would be a reasonable maximum size to allow in the elements of the array SHIP.

## A caution

Regardless of whether you are dealing with constants, simple variables, or arrays and their elements, it is important to realise that only character values may be assigned to character variables, and that character values may only be assigned to character variables.

So, SHIP (25) = 4 makes no sense at all, because the elements of the array SHIP have to be 15-character strings, and 4 is an integer: the two are quite incompatible. SHIP(25) = '4' would be quite all right, and would result in

```
SHIP(25)    4 _ _ _ _ _ _ _ _ _ _ _ _ _ _
```

In the same way, to write NSHIP = 4 is quite acceptable; it is the assignment of the integer value 4 to the integer variable NSHIP. But it would be entirely wrong to have written NSHIP = '4', since a character string may not be assigned to a numeric variable. It is important to try to keep similar types together.

## Substrings

If we have a string (for brevity, and in line with common practice, the simpler term 'string' rather than 'character string' will be used) we can select any part of that string – a *substring* – by using a simple notation. The individual characters of a string are considered to be numbered consecutively, starting at 1, from left to right. In the string 'LOVE, OH LOVE, OH CARELESS LOVE', the 'L' of the second 'LOVE' is in character position 10, and the 'E' of the same word is in position 13. Given the declaration

```
CHARACTER LINE * 40, WORD * 10
```

and the assignment

```
LINE = 'LOVE, OH LOVE, OH CARELESS LOVE'
```

we can select that particular word by means of the statement

```
WORD = LINE(10:13)
```

and the result will be

```
WORD      L O V E _ _ _ _ _ _
```

The two numbers in parentheses specify the limits of the substring.

In general, $(i:j)$ means 'the substring consisting of the $i$th to the $j$th character, inclusive'. As is the case with subscripts, we can use any integer expression to indicate a substring bound. The following fragment counts the occurrences of the substring 'OV' in the string LINE. We assume N to be the length of the string, ignoring trailing spaces.

```
      ...
      KOUNT = 0
      DO 10 I = 1,N-1
        IF (LINE(I:I+1).EQ.'OV') KOUNT = KOUNT + 1
   10 CONTINUE
      PRINT *, '"OV" APPEARS ', KOUNT, ' TIMES.'
      ...
```

We could have determined the length of LINE like this:

```
      ...
      DO 20 LENGTH = 40,0,-1
        IF (LINE(LENGTH:LENGTH).NE.' ') GO TO 30
   20 CONTINUE
      LENGTH = LENGTH + 1
   30 PRINT *, LINE, ' CONTAINS ', LENGTH,
      *            ' CHARACTERS.'
      ...
```

The loop is counting backwards from the end of the string, seeking a non-space character. Note the need for correction if the string contains all spaces and the DO loop terminates naturally. Obviously, a substring consisting of a single character is selected by giving the lower and upper bounds the same value.

Either bound may be omitted, in which case a default value is assumed: in the case of the lower bound, the default is 1; for a missing upper bound, the default is the string length. Hence,

LINE(:13) is 'LOVE, OH LOVE'

and

LINE(19:) is 'CARELESS LOVE                ' (note the trailing spaces)

If both bounds are omitted, the whole string is used. LINE(:) is equivalent to LINE.

## Comparison of strings

As the second fragment shows, simple comparisons between strings are quite simple. If the strings are the same length, the relations .EQ. and .NE. can safely be used to test for equality or otherwise. If the strings differ in length, the comparison is performed as though the shorter of the two strings had been extended with spaces at the right-hand end.

We *can* use the other relational operators (.LT., .LE., .GE., .GT.) but this needs a little more care, since there is no universally agreed ordering of characters. There *are* standards, but no single standard. Normally, of course, we would regard 'A' as less than 'B', which in turn is less than 'C', etc. In the same way (bearing in mind that we are considering *characters*, not numbers), it does not seem unreasonable that we should regard '0' (zero) as less than '1', '1' as less than '2', etc. This natural ordering is also built into FORTRAN 77. In addition, it is specified that the 'space' character is both less than 'A' and less than '0'. But we are given no guidance as to the relative ordering of '9' and 'A', '0' and 'Z'. Different computers may, therefore, produce different results when asked to place, for example, 'ABC3' and 'ABCD' in order. If the letters precede the digits in the machine's *collating sequence* (character ordering 'built in' to the machine by virtue of the internal numerical representation of characters) we shall get

    ABCD
    ABC3

If the digits precede the letters, we shall get

    ABC3
    ABCD

Introducing any other characters causes yet more problems. This table shows the order of a 48-character subset of characters when using the extended binary-coded interchange code (EBCDIC) or the American standard code for information interchange (ASCII), two of the more commonly encountered character-coding systems.

| EBCDIC | ASCII | |
|--------|-------|---|
| 'space' | 'space' | |
| . | $ | |
| ( | ' | (quote) |
| + | ( | |
| $ | ) | |
| * | * | |
| ) | + | |
| − | , | (comma) |
| / | − | |

| EBCDIC | | ASCII | |
|---|---|---|---|
| , | (comma) | . | |
| = | | / | |
| ' | (quote) | 0 | (zero) |
| A | | 1 | |
| B | | . . . | |
| . . . | | 9 | |
| Z | | = | |
| 0 | (zero) | A | |
| . . . | | . . . | |
| 9 | | Z | |

Both satisfy the FORTRAN 77 requirements, but the differences are great. There is virtually no relationship between the order of special characters; in EBCDIC, letters precede digits, in ASCII the reverse is true; the '=' character precedes both letters and digits in EBCDIC, in common with the other special characters, but it comes *between* the digits and the letters in ASCII. Obviously, then, if one is comparing anything other than purely alphabetic or purely numeric data, there is a need to be aware of one's machine's collating sequence. This means, often, that a program that works on one computer will fail – or produce different results, which is usually the same thing – if it is used on a different machine. For what would seem to be purely selfish commercial reasons, computer manufacturers have so far been unable to agree on a single collating sequence applicable to all machines.

## Character functions

As a move towards improving this situation, FORTRAN 77 offers its users four 'lexical comparison' functions. We have already met the MOD function, in Chapter 5, and we shall soon see that there are many more, but the ones we shall consider immediately are specifically designed to handle strings, and each produces a LOGICAL result – either .TRUE. or .FALSE. The four functions are:

| | |
|---|---|
| `LLT(X, Y)` | .TRUE. if x is lexically less than y |
| `LLE(X, Y)` | .TRUE. if x is lexically not greater than y |
| `LGE(X, Y)` | .TRUE. if x is lexically not less than y |
| `LGT(X, Y)` | .TRUE. if x is lexically greater than y |

In all other circumstances, the value .FALSE. is produced. X and Y are character variables or constants.

These functions may only be used in expressions on the right-hand side of an assignment statement; in other statements, they can appear wherever a LOGICAL expression is appropriate.

A lexical comparison is performed character by character from left to right and is based on the ASCII collating sequence. Thus 'ABC3' is less than 'ABCD', and 'PETER' is less then 'PETER RABBIT', after due allowance for the right-padding, with blanks, of 'PETER'.

**Examples**

(a) LLT('BO', 'PEEP') is .TRUE.
(b) CHARACTER * 5 A, B, C * 11
    LOGICAL QUERY, ASK
    . . .
    C = 'ALL''S WELL'
    A = 'ALL'
    B = C(1:3)
    QUERY = LLE(A, B) makes QUERY .TRUE.
    . . .
(c) but
    ASK = LGT(C(8:11), 'WHALE') makes ASK .FALSE.
(d) CHARACTER FLAG
    . . .
    IF (LGE(FLAG, 'N')) THEN
      PRINT *, 'SECOND HALF'
    ELSE
      PRINT *, 'FIRST HALF'
    END IF
    . . .

Here, we compare the single character in FLAG with 'N'. If it is equal to or greater than 'N', we print 'SECOND HALF', which is the part of the alphabet it is in, if it is indeed alphabetic. Otherwise we print 'FIRST HALF'.

Several other functions are of interest when handling characters. Here are their descriptions.

LEN(X) returns the length of the character item X.

**Examples**

(a) L = LEN('FRED') gives the value 4 to L
(b) CHARACTER PETE * 5, JOE * 7
    . . .
    K = LEN(JOE) + LEN(PETE) − 1 gives K the value 11

INDEX(P, Q) gives the position of the first occurrence of the substring Q in the string P. If Q does not appear in P, the value zero is returned.

**Examples** (based on the earlier 'CARELESS LOVE' example)

(a) `I = INDEX(LINE, 'CARELESS')`

would give I the value 19, since the first character of the substring 'CARELESS' appears at position 19 in the string LINE.

(b) A two-character string is read in, and the number of its occurrences in LINE is determined and printed. An additional declaration is needed: `CHARACTER * 2 SST`

```
      ...
      READ *, SST
      KOUNT = 0
      I = 1
      K = INDEX(LINE(I:), SST)
C         THIS CHECKS FROM POSITION I ONWARD
C         FOR AN OCCURRENCE OF SST
   10 IF (K .NE. 0) THEN
      KOUNT = KOUNT + 1
C         AFTER INCREASING THE COUNT, CONTINUE THE
C         SCAN, BUT MOVE THE START POINT ONE PLACE
C         BEYOND THE MATCH POINT

      I = K + 1
      K = INDEX(LINE(I:), SST)
      GO TO 10
      ELSE
      PRINT *, '''', SST, ''' OCCURS ', KOUNT, ' TIMES.'
      END IF
      ...
```

The output will be, if the input is 'ov'

```
'OV' OCCURS 3 TIMES.
```

Note the use of ' ' to obtain a single quote on output.

ICHAR(X) is a function that delivers the position of the single character denoted by X in the collating sequence of the machine being used. The position of the *first* character in the collating sequence is 0; if the sequence contains a total of N characters, the position of the last one is (N-1).

ICHAR, then, enables us to obtain a unique integer value associated with each character. On the other hand, CHAR(I) is a function whose value is a *character* – the one that is at position I in the collating sequence.

**Example**

Assuming that there are at least 64 characters in the collating sequence of whatever machine you are using, this fragment should print out the first 64 characters of the machine's collating sequence:

```
      DO 10 I = 0, 63
         PRINT *, CHAR(I)
   10 CONTINUE
      END
```

## Concatenation

One of the operations most frequently applied to strings is that of *concatenation*. This simply means joining one string onto the end of another. Because it is so useful, we have a special FORTRAN 77 operator denoted by a double slash, //. This operator can only be applied to CHARACTER type data. Thus, 'FRED' // 'DIE' is equivalent to 'FREDDIE', because // causes 'DIE' to be joined on to the end of 'FRED'.

**Examples**

(a) Suppose that STR1 and STR2 have been declared as CHARACTER * 4.

```
STR1 = 'P' / / 'Q' / / 'R'       makes STR1 P Q R␣
STR2 = STR1(3:4) / /'XY'         makes STR2 R␣X Y
```

Note that concatenation cannot make a CHARACTER variable any bigger than it was when declared:

```
STR1 = STR2 / / '*'     makes STR1 R␣X Y
```

– the excess character is just lost.

(b) This little routine reads in three names, inserts spaces between them and prints the full name.

```
CHARACTER * 15 FIRST, MIDDLE, LAST, NAME * 50
READ *, FIRST, MIDDLE, LAST
NAME = FIRST / / ' ' / / MIDDLE / / ' ' / / LAST
PRINT *, NAME
END
```

Concatenation needs a little care in its use, because it is not permitted to have on the right of an assignment a substring of the string named on the left-hand side.

Thus,

```
Q = 'ARTHUR' / / Q(10:19)
```

would be invalid.

## Exercises

Write programs to perform the following tasks.

1 Read in three 10-character strings and print them out in lexicographical order.
2 Read in a word (up to 15 characters) and print it out with the letters reversed. Can you avoid the output of unwanted leading spaces in the output? (They are a result of a word containing fewer than 15 letters.)
3 The array LINE contains 80 single characters. A word within LINE is defined as any sequence of characters terminated by either a space or a full stop. Count the number of words in LINE.
4 The 80-character string PLAIN is to be encoded to give another 80-character string CODE. This is to be achieved by converting each alphabetic character of PLAIN into the character that is exactly five positions further on in the alphabet, with 'wrap-around' where necessary. Thus, 'A' becomes 'F', 'B' becomes 'G', 'U' becomes 'Z', and then 'V' becomes 'A', 'W' becomes 'B' and so on. The non-alphabetic characters are to be transmitted unchanged. The message 'BOXING DAY, 1982' will be encoded as 'GTCNSL IFD, 1982'.

# 9

# Functions

Computer programs are usually developed in 'chunks' of self-contained code called *modules*, or *program units* in FORTRAN. There are a number of different kinds of program unit, and the sort that we have been talking about so far is called a *main program*.

Early on in the book, the development of computing over the past 35 years or so was briefly covered. In particular, we mentioned the ideas and improvements that have produced high-level languages, such as FORTRAN. In the early days of programming, each operation had to be coded individually, and a feature that we now take for granted on even the smallest microcomputer system – such as division – required complex sequences of machine-language instructions. Later, autocodes made their appearance, and such sequences could then be expressed by a single code word, or symbol.

What had happened was that someone had realised that all divisions (or whatever the process might be) are very much the same, and that if the basic set of machine instructions that does the task is stored away somewhere in the machine it can be recovered and inserted at the appropriate point in the program when a trigger word, such as 'DIVIDE', appears in the source program. Alternatively, to save memory space, a branch to the stored routine could be inserted into the program at that point, and a return made to the main – or, rather, calling – program when the work had been done.

Such sets of instructions intended for general use were called *subroutines*, and they are widely used in all programming systems, including FORTRAN. In FORTRAN, we speak of program units called *subprograms*, which are separately compiled procedures designed to do specific jobs when invoked (called into action) by another program unit. The two main types are the *function subprogram* and the *subroutine subprogram*. We have met some functions already, so let us consider them first. There are, in fact, several types.

## Intrinsic functions

Extraction of a square root is an arithmetic operation that is needed quite frequently. The time, in seconds, for the complete swing of a simple pendulum is given by the formula

$$t = 2\pi \sqrt{\frac{l}{g}}$$

where $l$ is the length of the pendulum in centimetres; $g$ is the gravitational constant (981 cm sec$^{-2}$).

The problem here is that we need to compute a square root. However, we do not need to write the rather involved set of instructions that would achieve this objective – it has been done for us, and the instructions are held in the computer's mathematical 'library', together with many other prospectively useful routines. All we need to know is the name of the routine and use it in our arithmetic expression, thus:

```
T = 2 * 3.14159265 * SQRT( L / G )
```

The magic word here is 'SQRT' – an obvious abbreviation of the words '<u>s</u>quare <u>root</u>'. The quantity whose square root is to be calculated is called the *argument* and the expression representing that argument is contained in parentheses. Putting the word 'SQRT' in front of the parentheses causes the enclosed expression to be evaluated and then its square root to be computed. The value so determined is then used in the complete calculation.

The following program computes and prints a table of numbers and their square roots, from 1 to 10.

```
      DO 10 I = 1, 10
        RI = I
        ROOT = SQRT(RI)
        PRINT *, I, ROOT
   10 CONTINUE
      END
```

There is a certain amount of redundancy in this program, in that one may use arithmetic expressions in the PRINT statement. But the statement 'RI =I' is not part of the redundancy; SQRT may not be used with an integer argument, so the value of I has to be converted to a real value. This is most simply done by assigning it to a real variable, RI. Another way to achieve the same effect would be to use another intrinsic function: the expression 'REAL(I)' computes the real value corresponding to the argument I. If we do this, the program shrinks somewhat:

```
      DO 10 I = 1, 10
         PRINT *, I, SQRT(REAL(I))
   10 CONTINUE
      END
```

This is an example of nesting one function call inside another. When this is done, the most deeply nested functions are evaluated first, because it is necessary to determine the values of the arguments before a function can be applied to them.

A function is a procedure that computes a single value. It is worth noting that it does not *do* anything with that value; in effect, it delivers it to the expression in which the function name appears as though it were just another subexpression – which, in fact, it is. So, for instance, the expression SQRT(RI) does not *change* the value of RI; it *uses* that value to calculate another one – its square root.

If the argument of SQRT happens to be negative, the effect is undefined. Most computer systems will report an error condition and terminate the execution of the program that caused the fault. In general, it is best to test the argument before applying the SQRT function, to ensure that it is not negative; if it *does* happen to be negative, you can then take whatever seems to be the appropriate action before failure occurs. This is another example of the programmer retaining control of his program. Like this:

```
  . . .
  IF (X .GE. 0.0) THEN
     Y = SQRT(X)
  ELSE
     PRINT *, 'NEGATIVE SQUARE ROOT ARGUMENT ', X
     STOP
  END IF
  . . .
```

One would hope, in practice, to be a little more specific about the error and the point in the program at which it occurs in order to give the user the best possible chance of pinpointing the fault and correcting it. Something like this might be better:

```
. . .
  PRINT *, ' *** ERROR 123 ***'
  PRINT *, ' ATTEMPT TO TAKE . . .', X
. . .
```

The user needs a document which suggests possible corrective actions if ERROR 123 is reported.

FORTRAN 77 has some 40 intrinsic functions defined for the convenience of its users. Here is a selection of them.

### EXP

The FORTRAN statement

```
Y = EXP(X)
```

is equivalent to the algebraic expression

$$y = e^x$$

in which $e$ is the base of natural logarithms. This *exponential function* is used a great deal in scientific and engineering calculations. The argument, $x$, must not be an INTEGER value.

### LOG

This is a function used to compute the natural logarithm of its argument.

```
Y = LOG(X)
```

is the FORTRAN equivalent of

$$y = ln\ x \ (or\ y = \log_e x)$$

Again, the argument must not be of INTEGER type, nor must it be negative. If the logarithm to base 10 is required, the function name is LOG10:

```
Y = LOG10(X)
```

gives us $y = \log_{10} x$

## Trigonometric functions – SIN, COS, TAN

These are mathematical functions of angles and, when used in FORTRAN, the angles must be expressed in radians. There are $2\pi$ radians in a circle (i.e. 360 degrees). It follows that to convert degrees to radians it is necessary to multiply by $\frac{\pi}{360}$, approximately 0.01745. For those readers who have forgotten their trigonometry, Fig. 9.1 may act as a reminder.

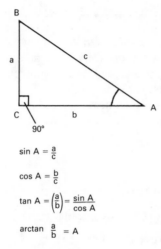

$$\sin A = \frac{a}{c}$$

$$\cos A = \frac{b}{c}$$

$$\tan A = \left(\frac{a}{b}\right) = \frac{\sin A}{\cos A}$$

$$\text{arctan } \frac{a}{b} = A$$

**Fig. 9.1**

## Inverse trigonometric functions – ASIN, ACOS, ATAN

These functions, given as argument a sine, cosine or tangent, respectively, produce the corresponding angle, expressed in radians.

The trigonometric and inverse trigonometric functions should not have INTEGER arguments.

**ABS**

This is a function used to determine the absolute value of its argument, that is, the magnitude of it without regard to sign. For example, ABS(10) and ABS(−10) will both produce the same result, +10; and ABS(32.2) will produce the same result as ABS(−32.2), namely +32.2. The argument may be integer or real, and the result is of the same type as the argument.

A typical application might be in finding the square root of a difference, representing a length, that may turn out to be negative:

```
DIST = SQRT(ABS(X**2 − Y**2))
```

## Type conversion functions – INT and REAL

It is occasionally convenient to convert an integer value to the equivalent real form, or vice versa, and these functions enable the conversion to be performed. If one wants the true quotient of a pair of integer values, for example, one of them must be converted to type REAL, at least, if truncation is to be avoided. In such a case, an assignment such as the following would be used:

```
QUOT = REAL(N)/M
```

An alternative is:

```
QUOT = N/REAL(M)
```

or even (though rather overdoing it):

```
QUOT = REAL(N) / REAL(M)
```

If N has the value 9 and M has the value 5, the result in each of these cases would be to assign the value 1.8 to QUOT. But remember the rule about evaluating the argument first. This one gives the wrong answer:

```
QUOT = REAL(N/M)
```

The reason is that the value of N/M is computed first and, with the normal integer truncation on division, this produces a result of 1 which, when converted by the REAL function, produces a final value assigned to QUOT of 1.0.

It is not usually possible to convert a real value to an integer without losing something through truncation, unless the real value happens to represent a whole number. But one would often like the *integer part* of a real value, and the INT conversion function enables us to obtain this in INTEGER form. We have, of course, the MOD function for obtaining the remainder of a division, as we saw in an earlier chapter, but we can get the same result in this way:

```
REM = X — Y * INT(X/Y)
```

This is for real values of X and Y, of course. For two integers, one need only write.

```
IREM = J — K * (J/K)*
```

If the truncated value is wanted in REAL form, there is a special function called AINT that will provide it. Thus, to avoid conversion to integer and the necessary reconversion implied in the first example above, one would write, in practice.

```
REM = X — Y * AINT(X/Y)
```

## Rounding

There are two functions that give the nearest whole number value to an argument of REAL type. NINT produces an INTEGER type result; for a REAL type result the function ANINT is used. The method used is to calculate, for either NINT or ANINT, the value int$(x + 0.5)$ if the argument $x$ is not less than zero, or int$(x - 0.5)$ if $x$ is negative. These functions thus enable a rounded value to be computed.

## Maxima and minima

The functions MAX and MIN are unusual in that the number of arguments they may have is unspecified. MAX delivers the largest of its arguments, MIN delivers the smallest of its arguments, in the

---

* Note the need to parenthesise (J/K) to ensure the truncating division is carried out before the multiplication. Try it for yourself to see the difference between

$17 - 5 * (17 / 5)$ and $17 - 5 * 17 / 5$

The first produces the correct answer, 2, the second gives 0. We could, in this case, have avoided the problem by writing the expression in a different order: $17 - 17 / 5 * 5$ gives the correct answer without parentheses. But it all shows that you need to be a little bit careful.

algebraic sense. Thus, if A = 3.1, B = 4.1, C = 5.9, D = 2.6, E = 5.0, the expression

```
MAX(A, B, C, D, E)
```

would have the value 5.9, and

```
MIN(A, B, C, D, E)
```

would produce 2.6.

All the arguments must be of the same type, and the result is also of that type. Sometimes, a result of the other type is wanted, in which case the type conversion functions should be used:

```
INT(MAX(A, B, C, D, E))
```

will produce the value 5, and

```
REAL(MIN(2, 1, 7, 4, −3, 6))
```

will produce the value −3.0.

There are a number of other functions available, and a number of their features not detailed here. A full list is given in Appendix A.

## Functions defined by the programmer

The user of FORTRAN has available to him a good selection of intrinsic functions, as the previous sections will have indicated, but it is not possible in this way to provide for every need of all users. Facilities are therefore provided to enable users to define functions to meet their own individual requirements. The simplest of these is the *statement function*.

## Statement functions

Often, a program unit will require that a particular calculation be performed a number of times, not in a regular sequence, as might be the case if a loop were used, but at various points in the program, scattered rather irregularly. For example, the distance of a point from the origin of coordinate axes is given by the formula

$$d = \sqrt{x^2 + y^2}$$

where the coordinates of the point are $(x, y)$. If there are several different points to be considered, with coordinates held in different variables, or computed by a variety of formulae, one might find the following statements scattered around the program unit:

```
DIST = SQRT(X1**2 + Y1**2)
SEP = 10.5 - SQRT(P**2 + ABS(Q - R)**2)
Z = SQRT(A**2 + B**2) + SQRT(A**2 + C**2)
```

All of these statements involve the evaluation of an expression in which two values are squared and added, after which the square root of the resulting value is extracted. There is no reason why we should not write these formulae in the program, exactly as they appear here, each time they are wanted. The resulting program would be efficient, but there is always the danger that there could be some miscopying – perhaps a minus sign where a plus is intended, for instance, which would lead to the production of wrong answers and might be quite difficult to locate when the error was noticed. It is also rather time-consuming to have to copy out the formula with different arguments each time, especially if it is at all complicated.

An alternative is to reduce the effort required, and possibly make rather more efficient use of the machine's memory capacity, by writing out the calculation *once only*. We could then give the code a name and use it as though we were calling an intrinsic function into action, leaving the machine to substitute the appropriate variables in the correct places, having provided them in the form of a list of arguments. We do this by defining a statement function. There are two restrictions that need to be borne in mind: the calculation specified must be capable of expression by means of *a single FORTRAN statement* and, secondly, it can only be used within the program unit in which it is defined.

Having decided to write a statement function, such as one for our distance formula, we need to choose a unique name for it. Unlike the names of some of the intrinsic functions we have considered, the name of a programmer-defined function is constructed in accordance with the normal conventions as to type. The first letter of the name, unless there is a type declaration for the name, will determine the type of the result that is produced. For an INTEGER result, the name will normally start with the letter I, J, K, L, M or N; for a REAL result, one of the remaining letters of the alphabet. Our function will produce a real result, so we could safely call it DSTNCE.

It needs to know the coordinates of the point whose distance from the origin is to be calculated, so it will have two arguments. These will also be real values. We do not know what the names of these values will be when the programmer uses the function – indeed, they can be any real expression, but we shall have to use something to represent them in our definition. These are called *dummy arguments*, and we shall use x and y in our example. If you like, these can be regarded as labels for 'holes' in a template, which will be filled by the *actual arguments* when the function is used. The names are unimportant, and may be reused, without fear of confusion, before and after the definition of the statement function – they are said to be *local* to the definition.

The next step is to write the definition, which will specify the general form of the calculation in terms of the dummy arguments.

```
DSTNCE(X, Y) = SQRT(X**2 + Y**2)
```

Once this is done – and the definition must appear at the head of the program unit and may only be followed by either the first executable statement of the unit or another statement function definition – we can rewrite the three statements given at the start of this section, as follows:

```
DIST = DSTNCE(X1, Y1)
SEP = 10.5 - DSTNCE(P, ABS(Q - R))
Z = DSTNCE(A, B) + DSTNCE(A, C)
```

This is not only simpler, but arguably more descriptive of what is happening. We have abstracted the essential feature of the action in the name of the function: the third example might be read as 'z is the distance to (A, B) plus the distance to (A, C)'. When the statement that calls the function is encountered during the execution of the program, the effect is as though the definition's right-hand side were substituted for the function reference, with each dummy argument replaced by the corresponding actual argument.

It is important to realise that the relation of the actual arguments to the dummy arguments is established purely by their position within the parentheses. There must be agreement in the order, type and number of arguments. It would be quite wrong, for instance, to call DSTNCE with a statement such as

```
W = DSTNCE(P, Q, R, S)
```

since there are more actual arguments than dummy arguments. In the same way,

```
D = DSTNCE(I, J)
```

is wrong because the arguments in the calling statement are of integer type, and the dummy arguments of the definition are real.

```
V = DSTNCE(K, A, B)
```

would be wrong on both counts.

A statement function definition may refer to other statement functions, as long as they have been defined previously.

The final example is based on the leap year example of Chapter 5.

This function produces a LOGICAL value, and so its name will need to appear in a LOGICAL type declaration:

```
      LOGICAL LEAPYR
      INTEGER YEAR
      LEAP(YEAR) = MOD(YEAR,100) .NE. 0 .AND.
     *             MOD(YEAR,  4) .EQ. 0
     *       .OR.  MOD(YEAR,100) .EQ. 0 .AND.
     *             MOD(YEAR,400) .EQ. 0
      . . .
```

This might then be used by such statements as

```
      IF LEAPYR(1984) THEN
        PRINT *, 'YOU HAVE A'
      ELSE
        PRINT *, 'YOU HAVE NO'
      END IF
      PRINT *, 'BIRTHDAY THIS YEAR.'
```

or

```
C       IN THIS EXAMPLE, THE COMPUTER IS A BEAUTIFUL
C       UNMARRIED LADY WHO WANTS TO CHOOSE HER OWN
C       HUSBAND.
      CHARACTER * 10 NAME, REPLY * 3
      LOGICAL LEAPYR, ELIGBL, MALE, MARRID
C       UNFORTUNATELY, SHE CAN ONLY PROPOSE IN A
C       LEAP YEAR. IN THE UNLIKELY EVENT THAT SHE
C       IS REFUSED, SHE MUST TRY AGAIN.
      INTEGER YEAR
      LEAPYR(YEAR) = . . . (definition as already given)
      READ *, YEAR
C       IS IT A LEAP YEAR?
      IF (LEAPYR(YEAR)) THEN
```

```
C       YES, IT IS.
  10    READ *, NAME
        IF (NAME .EQ. 'I GIVE UP') THEN
         PRINT *, 'SORRY, I COULDN'T BE SUITORED'
         STOP
        ELSE
         READ *, MALE, MARRID
         ELIGBL = MALE .AND. .NOT. MARRID
        END IF
        IF (.NOT. ELIGBL) GO TO 10
C       THIS LOOKS LIKE A CHANCE: PROPOSE!
        PRINT *, 'WILL YOU MARRY ME, ', NAME, '?'
        READ *, REPLY
        IF (REPLY .NE. 'YES') GO TO 10
        PRINT *, 'AND THEY LIVED HAPPILY EVER AFTER.'
       ELSE
C       OH, DEAR, IT ISN'T A LEAP YEAR.
C       WHEN IS THE NEXT ONE?
        DO 20 NEXT = YEAR+1, YEAR+7
        IF (LEAPYR(NEXT)) GO TO 30
  20    CONTINUE
C       ONE OF THOSE SEVEN MUST BE A LEAP YEAR,
C       BUT JUST IN CASE . . .
        PRINT *, 'ERROR: CAN''T FIND LEAP YEAR'
        STOP
  30    PRINT *, YEAR, ' IS NOT A LEAP YEAR.'
        PRINT *, 'TRY AGAIN IN ', NEXT, '.'
       END IF
       END
```

Apart from the uses of the statement function LEAPYR, note the use of CHARACTER and LOGICAL variables and comments. Some programmers will not like the way I have placed a STOP statement in the second THEN clause, but it seems the cleanest way to do it. Note how the statement READ *, MALE, MARRID brings in LOGICAL data. This can be input as T (for true) and F (for false). Note also the error message after statement number 20. There is no way that the loop can terminate naturally. Nevertheless, just in case we have overlooked something and it *does*, this message will tell us. This is better than running into the block that starts at statement number 30 by accident. Remember the cardinal laws of programming:

1 If anything can go wrong, it will.
2 Even if there is nothing to go wrong, something will.
3 When you have removed all the errors, there are still some left.

## Function subprograms

It is not always possible – indeed, it is quite rare – to be able to express the complete logic of a function as a single statement. The *function subprogram* is very similar in use to the statement function, but there are one or two fundamental differences. In the first place, while the statement function forms part of the program unit that uses it, and so is compiled as part of that program unit, a function subprogram is a quite independent program unit, compiled separately from the program unit that calls it. Secondly, a function subprogram may contain any number of FORTRAN statements, making it much more flexible and powerful than the simpler statement function.

Function subprograms are named in the same way as statement functions: the initial letter basically determines whether the result produced by the function is to be REAL or INTEGER.

The following is an example of a function subprogram that returns as its result the standard deviation of the first N elements of the array A. We assume that A has a maximum of 250 elements.

```
      FUNCTION STDEV(A, N)
      DIMENSION A(250)
      REAL MEAN
C         COMPUTE THE MEAN OF THE FIRST N VALUES
      SUM = 0.0
      DO 10 I = 1, N
        SUM = SUM + A(I)
   10 CONTINUE
      MEAN = SUM/N
C         NOW, THE SUM OF SQUARES OF DEVIATIONS
      SMSQDV = 0.0
      DO 20 I = 1, N
        SMSQDV = SMSQDV + (A(I) - MEAN)**2
   20 CONTINUE
      STDEV = SQRT(SMSQDV/(N - 1))
      RETURN
      END
```

There are only two new types of statement in this example: the FUNCTION statement, and the RETURN statement. Let us have a quick look at these before considering the code in more detail.

In FUNCTION STDEV(A, N), the word FUNCTION informs the compiler that a function subprogram is about to be defined. It will be referred to by the name STDEV and, since this is the name of a

REAL variable, we assume that the function will deliver a REAL result. Following the function name is a list of dummy arguments, enclosed in parentheses. When the function is invoked, these dummy arguments will, in effect, be replaced – wherever they appear in the function definition – by the actual arguments given in the calling statement.

When a subprogram is invoked, a link is established between the two program units (which were compiled separately, you will recall). This link serves to establish the connection between the actual and dummy arguments, and also specifies the exact point in the calling program from which the reference to the subprogram was made. This is called the *return address*, and the job of the RETURN statement is to extract this return address from wherever it was stored on entry to the subprogram and branch back into the calling routine at the instruction immediately after that which invoked the subprogram. Obviously, then, the RETURN statement will be the last one executed in the evaluation of a function. This is *not* the same as saying that it should be the last statement of the subprogram though, as it happens, that is the case in our example, apart from the END statement. Here, in fact, we could have omitted the RETURN, since an END statement encountered during the execution of a subprogram has exactly the same effect. But there may be several points within a subprogram from which one would like to return to the calling routine: at each of these points, one may place a RETURN statement, whereas no program unit may have more than one END statement, and that must be the very last.

Given that the formula for the sample standard deviation of the elements of the array A is

$$s = \sqrt{\frac{\sum_{i=1}^{n} (A_i - \bar{a})^2}{(n-1)}}$$

where $\bar{a}$ is the mean of the $n$ elements, the remainder of the subprogram becomes almost self-explanatory. Note, however, the statement

```
STDEV = SQRT(SMSQDV/(N - 1))
```

in which the required result is computed and assigned to a 'variable' that has the name of the function. This is an essential feature of all function subprograms – the final value must be assigned to the function in this way. The name of the function may be used just as though it were an ordinary variable: in this way, the result is returned to the calling routine. In the program that calls it, reference is made to the function in exactly the same way as if it were an intrinsic function, or a statement function. A typical call might be:

```
SDX = STDEV(X, 100)
```

This calculates the sample standard deviation of the first 100 elements of the array x. Again, it is necessary that the actual arguments (here, x and 100) agree in number, order and type with the dummy arguments (A and N).

Subscripted variables may be used inside a function subprogram, and care must be taken to ensure that any which do appear have appropriate DIMENSION or type statements at the head of the program unit. As we have seen, the dummy arguments may be the *names* of arrays, but they should not be subscripted – if you think about it, you will see that while it will often make sense to have a subscripted variable as an *actual* argument there is little point in subscripting a *dummy* argument, which is simply a name to be replaced by what we might term 'the real thing' when the program is run.

In the example, we allowed for the array A to have a maximum size of 250. If we had no idea of the number of elements A might have, we could have dimensioned it like this:

```
DIMENSION A(*)
```

which would have the effect of giving A the same number of elements as its corresponding actual argument at runtime. This can be very convenient, but needs a little care; only the right-most subscript can be treated in this way. The reason is to do with the way in which FORTRAN works out the memory addresses of the individual elements of arrays; the right-most subscript is not needed at the compilation stage, when the DIMENSION statement (or corresponding type statement) is processed and the storage organisation is being determined.

Arguments of type CHARACTER may also be used, and they may be represented by dummy arguments declared as either character variables or character arrays. The actual argument must not contain more characters than is specified for the corresponding dummy. Again, it is possible to ensure that, at runtime, the length attribute of the actual argument is used by declaring, in the function subprogram, an unspecified length for the dummy. The following is a function subprogram, which counts the number of digits in the character string that is its argument.

```
      FUNCTION NUMBER(DIGITS)
      CHARACTER * (*) DIGITS
      NUMBER = 0
      DO 10 K = 1, LEN(DIGITS)
        IF (DIGITS(K:K) .GE. '0' .AND.
    *       DIGITS(K:K) .LE. '9') THEN
          NUMBER = NUMBER + 1
        END IF
   10 CONTINUE
      END
```

The statement

```
      CHARACTER * (*) DIGITS
```

specifies that the dummy argument DIGITS is to take the length of the actual argument when the program is run.

Some economy might have been achieved, possibly with the loss of some readability, by computing the value of the Kth character in DIGITS once only in each loop:

```
  . . .
  DO 10 K = 1, LEN(DIGITS)
    CHAR = DIGITS(K:K)
    IF (CHAR .GE. '0' .AND. CHAR .LE. '9') THEN
      . . .
```

Another possibility would be to have used the lexical comparison functions:

```
      IF (LGE(CHAR, '0') .AND. LLE(CHAR, '9')) THEN
```

would then replace the IF statement given.

Note that if CHAR is introduced in this way, it will be necessary to declare it at the head of the function subprogram. Since CHAR is a single character, it will be sufficient to use a statement either before or after the declaration of DIGITS such as

```
      CHARACTER CHAR
```

Remember, the default length is one character. Alternatively, it could be combined with the declaration of DIGITS, but in that case we should have to make the length explicit.

```
CHARACTER * (*) DIGITS, CHAR * 1
```

Another, possibly neater, solution would be

```
CHARACTER DIGITS * (*), CHAR
```

or

```
CHARACTER CHAR, DIGITS * (*)
```

Personally, I like to keep the declarations of my dummy arguments and my local variables separate, however, and would opt for the first suggestion. Character arguments declared as * (*) may not be used as operands of the concatenation operator, except in an assignment to a character variable.

## The type of a function

Just as one can override the naming conventions that cause the compiler to assume that variable names beginning with the letters I through N are of INTEGER type and the others are of REAL type, by using the type declarators REAL, INTEGER, CHARACTER, LOGICAL (and one or two others, as we shall see later), so one can specify the type of a function, in the function declaration. The following function returns the value .TRUE. if its numerical argument (a REAL value) is negative, .FALSE. otherwise. It is, therefore, a LOGICAL function.

```
LOGICAL FUNCTION NGATIV(X)
NGATIV = .FALSE.
IF (X .LT. 0) NGATIV = .TRUE.
END
```

Unlike its predecessors, FORTRAN allows the type of a function to be declared inside the function subprogram, like that of any other variable. This is perhaps reasonable, since it is treated as such. The alternative approach is this:

```
FUNCTION NGATIV(X)
LOGICAL NGATIV
. . .
```

At this point, it should be emphasised that whenever the name of a function (apart from the intrinsics) departs from the conventional

REAL/INTEGER naming, the name of the function must appear in an appropriate type statement in every program unit that uses it. This applies to statement functions as well. It follows that any program unit that references NGATIV will need to have the declaration

```
LOGICAL NGATIV
```

in its heading. For example,

```
      PROGRAM CLSSFY
      LOGICAL NGATIV
      DO 10 I = 1, 50
        READ *, VALUE
        IF (NGATIV(VALUE)) PRINT *, I, VALUE,
     *                               ' IS NEGATIVE.'
   10 CONTINUE
      END
```

which reads in 50 numbers, printing out the position in the list and the value of those that are negative.

If this were not done, bearing in mind that each program unit is compiled as a separate entity, the compiler would think that NGATIV was of INTEGER type and produce a diagnostic message after the IF statement.

Just to demonstrate that there is more than one way to solve most problems, the same effect can be obtained by the use of a statement function such as this:

```
NGATIV(X) = X .LT. 0
```

It would need to be preceded by a declaration

```
LOGICAL NGATIV
```

and, of course, would be valid only for the routine in which it is placed. Nevertheless, this use of the logical expression is much neater, and we could rewrite the function subprogram using the same idiom:

```
      FUNCTION NGATIV(X)
      LOGICAL NGATIV
      NGATIV = X .LT. 0
      END
```

Once declared in this way, the subprogram may be used by any program unit in the FORTRAN 'job' (i.e. the complete set of program units submitted to the computer as a program to perform a specific task). Furthermore, functions declared as subprograms may be incorporated into the computer system's library of program units and used by any other job which needs that particular function. Such units are referred to as *external* functions, as opposed to the *intrinsic* functions that are built into the system from the moment of its inception.

## Functions as arguments of other functions

Just occasionally, it is necessary or convenient to write a subprogram that calls a function, but one wants to give the person using the subprogram the opportunity to specify what that function will be. Suppose, for example, that one had a function called CUREA, which calculates the area under a curve. It is unlikely that one would want to be specific about precisely what the curve was to be. Rather, one would write in general terms and allow the user to choose for himself. Thus the function might have a heading such as

```
FUNCTION CUREA(FN, LOWX, HIGHX, ERCODE)

REAL LOWX
INTEGER ERCODE
```

and be invoked by a statement such as

```
AREA = CUREA(POLY, 1.0, 2.0, K)
```

POLY is the *actual* argument, the name of a function that generates the values defining the curve and corresponds to the *dummy* argument FN. LOWX and HIGHX define the $x$ values between which the area is to be determined and are given actual values of 1.0 and 2.0. K is the actual variable to receive the error code that CUREA will allocate to the dummy argument ERCODE. The details of CUREA need not concern us, but the statement

```
Y = FN(X)
```

or something like it, will appear somewhere in the subprogram. This will be interpreted as though it were, in our example,

```
Y = POLY(X)
```

and will thus obtain a value of the function we wish to be used.

## The EXTERNAL statement

When that statement

```
AREA = CUREA(POLY, 1.0, 2.0, K)
```

is compiled, it is impossible for the compiler to deduce that POLY is the name of an external function rather than that of a simple REAL variable. But, if it is to generate the correct sequence of instructions, it does need that information. So we have to make sure that it gets it – that is a responsibility of the programmer. It is done by including a list of the names of external functions used as arguments of other functions, preceded by the word EXTERNAL. Note that this is done in the *calling* program unit. In our example, the statement will be

```
EXTERNAL POLY
```

It will be at the head of the program unit, among the other declarations, and the compiler will now have all the information it needs.

## The INTRINSIC statement

We could have called CUREA in this way:

```
A = CUREA(SIN, 0.0, 6.28, IERR)
```

where SIN is the intrinsic function that determines the sine of an angle. One of the oddities of FORTRAN (or one of its invaluable features, depending on your point of view) is that there are no 'reserved' words. So if you wish to define a function called SIN, or ABS or MOD or whatever, you are permitted to do so. The compiler does not get confused, because the names you choose take precedence over those that are built in, on the principle of 'last in, first out'. If you choose the name of an intrinsic function, therefore, the proper intrinsic becomes in effect invisible. It can no longer be accessed. Occasionally, this is useful, but it does present the programmer and compiler with a problem or two. Let us reconsider our example. Suppose we include the statement

```
EXTERNAL SIN
```

This is intended to signify that SIN is a function name used as an actual argument. The trouble here is the word EXTERNAL. The compiler will interpret the statement as meaning that SIN is an external (i.e. user-defined) function, with the same name as the intrinsic function SIN. The intrinsic thus becomes invisible from this point onward in this program unit! Now the problems appear:

1 All references to SIN in this program unit will be treated as referring to an external function – *not* the intrinsic. This is just the opposite of what we want!
2 When the program has compiled, and the system attempts to load its constituent program units into memory, it is very unlikely that SIN will be found as an external function since the programmer did not write it. An error condition will result.

So it cannot be done that way. Instead we use a statement, which is quite explicit and states that SIN, in this case, is the name of an intrinsic function:

    INTRINSIC SIN·

We do need to be rather careful in using the 'functions as arguments' approach, however, because some intrinsics may not be used as actual arguments. The following is a list of the forbidden names:

| AMAXO | DBLE | IFIX | MAX | REAL |
|-------|------|------|------|------|
| AMAX1 | DMAX1 | INT | MAXO | SNGL |
| AMINO | DMIN1 | LGE | MAX1 | |
| AMIN1 | FLOAT | LGT | MIN | |
| CHAR | ICHAR | LLE | MINO | |
| CMPLX | IDINT | LLT | MIN1 | |

This seems like a lot of exceptions to remember, but in fact consists of three well-defined groups of functions: the lexical comparisons, the type convertors and those that determine largest or smallest values. There are several in the list that we have not previously encountered.

## Specific versus generic intrinsic function names

Earlier FORTRAN systems had the same system of intrinsic functions as FORTRAN 77. The rule was invariable, however, that the name of a function should be an indicator of the type of result it produced. This was essentially a rule to help the compiler rather than the programmer and led to one's having to remember a lot of different intrinsic names, even when the same basic operation was to be performed. For example, consider the absolute value function: we would use ABS(x) for the absolute value of a REAL expression, but IABS(K) for the absolute value of an INTEGER expression.

As we shall see, the precision with which REAL values are represented in the computer can be increased considerably by specifying such values to be of DOUBLE PRECISION type. FORTRAN can also handle complex numbers, if they are declared as of COMPLEX type. This leads to two more functions: DABS(x) for the absolute value of a DOUBLE PRECISION expression and CABS(x) for the absolute value of a COMPLEX expression. We thus had four different names for the absolute value function, and the same was true of many of the others.

These names are still valid in FORTRAN 77 and may be used if you wish. They are called the *specific* names of the functions, because the name indicates the type of argument expected and that of the result produced.

However, it seems a little odd to have so many different names for what is essentially the same operation – in this case, the determination of an absolute value. Usually, the compiler has enough information available to be able to determine the type of the arguments and deduce the type of result to be produced. Where this is the case, a single function name can be used, regardless of the argument and result types. This is called the *generic* name of the function because it is wider ranging – it has more general application. Many functions have generic names; that for the absolute value function is ABS. Full details are given in Appendix A.

So far, we have stuck to the use of the generic function names in our examples, and it is recommended that you do the same whenever you can. HOWEVER . . . (and here we return to the point from which we have somewhat digressed) actual arguments that are the names of intrinsic functions must bear the *specific* function name. Unless this is done, since the compiler does not know what arguments will be used when the function is applied inside the function being called, the compiler will be unable to determine the particular 'variation' of the function to pass over to the called routine. So, in this case, you must be *specific*.

## Functions without arguments

We occasionally come across a case in which a function has no need of any arguments. Even so – for the convenience of the compiler – the parentheses that would enclose the argument list, if there was one, must be written. The following function reads one real number from the standard input device:

```
FUNCTION INREAL()
REAL INREAL
READ *, X
INREAL = X
END
```

It might be invoked by a sequence such as:

```
      . . .
C        CALCULATE THE AREA OF A TRIANGLE
C        GIVEN THE HEIGHT AND THE BASE LENGTH,
C        READ IN THAT ORDER FROM THE
C        STANDARD INPUT DEVICE
   AREA = 0.5*INREAL()*INREAL()
      . . .
```

This is obviously not the way to write programs of great clarity! It might be better to call the function twice:

```
. . .
HEIGHT = INREAL()
BASE = INREAL()
AREA = 0.5*HEIGHT*BASE
. . .
```

It still is not the clearest of programs. In this case the simple approach is probably the best, but the point is made: functions do not have to have arguments, but the parentheses – odd though they look – are needed.

## Exercises

1 Write down in your own words the rules for naming functions.

2 What are the essential differences between statement functions and function subprograms?

3 The formula

$$\frac{1}{f} = \frac{1}{u} + \frac{1}{v}$$

is to be evaluated (to give $f$) at a number of points in a program using different variables for '$u$' and '$v$' each time. Write a suitable FORTRAN function. Why did you choose that particular type of function?

4 A function called KOMPAR is required that compares its two integer arguments and returns the value $-1$ if the first is less than the second, 0 if they are equal, and $+1$ if the first is greater then the second. Write the appropriate function subprogram.

5 The function GET(S, I, T) takes the Ith symbol from the array S (each element of S is a string of six characters) and places it in the left-most position of the character variable T, which is then right-filled with space characters. T holds six characters. The final value returned by GET is the value of T. Write the function GET.

6 True or false?
   (a) Functions must always have arguments.
   (b) A function name may have up to six characters.
   (c) Intrinsic functions are written by the programmer for his own use.
   (d) When a function name is given as an argument for another function call, it must appear in the called function in an EXTERNAL statement.

# 10

# Subroutines

The second type of subprogram to be considered is the *subroutine*. Its structure differs from that of the function subprogram only in details, but it is used in quite a different way. The basic difference is in the way in which the results are returned to the calling program unit: a function is intended to produce a single value as its result, and this is returned in the name of the function; a subroutine is permitted to produce as many values as may be needed as results, and its name is *not* used for transmitting them. Further, whereas a function is called implicitly, by having its name and argument list appear in an appropriate expression, a subroutine must be called explicitly – a special FORTRAN statement is needed to initiate its actions. The results produced by a subroutine are transmitted back to the program unit that called it by means of the argument list. Nevertheless, the idea of a program unit that can stand alone, compiled separately from the calling routine, remains the same for subroutines as for functions.

**Example**
At a number of points in a program, it is required that the value and the position of the smallest element of an array shall be determined. Several different arrays of differing sizes are involved, though all are one-dimensional. Since two results are required, a function subprogram would not be suitable. The following is a subroutine subprogram to do the job.

```
SUBROUTINE SMALL(A, N, X, I)
```

```
C         A IS THE NAME OF THE ARRAY
C         N IS THE NUMBER OF ELEMENTS TO BE SCANNED
C         ON EXIT, X WILL CONTAIN
C         THE VALUE OF THE SMALLEST ELEMENT
C         I WILL INDICATE ITS POSITION IN THE ARRAY
          DIMENSION A(*)
C         DIMENSION A(N) WOULD HAVE BEEN EQUALLY SUITABLE
C         INITIALISE X AND I
          X = A(1)
          I = 1
C         EACH ELEMENT OF A IN TURN IS COMPARED
C         WITH X. WHEN A SMALLER VALUE IS FOUND,
C         THE VALUES OF X AND I ARE CHANGED APPROPRIATELY
          DO 10 NEXT = 2, N
          IF (A(NEXT) .LT. X) THEN
          X = A(NEXT)
          I = NEXT
          END IF
       10 CONTINUE
          RETURN
          END
```

Notice how the results are returned to the calling program; there are two arguments, x and i, which are given values during the execution of the subroutine. These are often called the 'output' arguments. This does not imply that anything is printed – just that these are what are produced. Similarly, the two arguments A and N give the subroutine the basic information it needs to perform its task. They are called the 'input' arguments of the subroutine or, more simply, its inputs. Again, it is not implied that a READ operation occurs. Sometimes, though not in this example, an argument will have its value changed by a subroutine. When this happens, it is called an 'input-output' argument. j, which is used only within the subroutine and cannot be referred to from outside the subroutine, is called a *local variable*.

The name of our example subroutine is SMALL. This is specified in the first statement of the subprogram, which must begin with the word SUBROUTINE followed by the name of the subprogram and, optionally, the argument list. This does not mean that the argument list can be omitted when there are arguments, but it does happen – rather more frequently than is the case for functions – that a subroutine does not need any. When this is the case, unlike the function, the parentheses that would enclose the arguments may also be omitted. The first statement of a subroutine subprogram (which will be called a subroutine, for brevity) must be a SUBROUTINE statement.

The subroutine is called into action from another program unit (never from within itself) by means of the CALL statement. For SMALL, this might typically be:

```
CALL SMALL(VALS, 100, RESULT, POSN)
```

in which it is assumed that POSN has been declared to be of INTEGER type. Again it will be seen that the actual arguments (in parentheses) agree in number, order and type with the dummy arguments of the subroutine. When the CALL statement is executed, control is passed to the first instruction of the subroutine. Wherever A is mentioned in the subroutine, VALS will be used; for X, RESULT will be understood; N and I will be effectively replaced by 100 and POSN, respectively. The subroutine will then be obeyed as though it were any other FORTRAN program. When either a RETURN statement or the terminal END statement is reached, control will be passed back to the calling routine at the statement immediately following the CALL statement. The values of RESULT and POSN will be those last assigned to X and I, respectively, in the subroutine. Note that the actual arguments may be any expression, but it would be foolish to use anything other than a variable or array element name for an output argument. Consider, for example, the following:

```
SUBROUTINE SWAP(A, B)
T = A
A = B
B = T
END
```

In this simple routine, T is a local variable. The purpose of the subprogram is to exchange the values of the two REAL variables A and B. Although it looks quite innocent, notice that A and B are input-output arguments: they both give *and receive* values. Thus, while a statement sequence such as

```
IF (P .LT. Q) THEN
  CALL SWAP(P, Q)
END IF
```

would be sensible and useful, something like

```
CALL SWAP(1.0, 2.0)
```

could cause confusion, and possibly chaos. Some computer systems would take this statement quite literally, with the effect that a later statement

```
Z = Z + 1.0
```

might cause the value of z to be increased by 2! Do not be tempted to do it.

The next example is of a simple subroutine without arguments. It has the effect of skipping 10 lines on the standard output device.

```
   SUBROUTINE SKIP10
   DO 10 I = 1, 10
   PRINT *
10 CONTINUE
   END
```

A suitable (indeed, the only possible) call for this subroutine would be

```
CALL SKIP10
```

Subroutines without arguments are not necessarily trivial. Later we shall see an example of one that is much more complex.

## Overall job structure

A FORTRAN *job* consists of exactly one main program and as many subprograms (functions or subroutines) as may be needed by the programmer. Usually, the main program will be positioned at the head of the job, so that it is compiled first. Subroutines and functions may appear in any order. In a very large job, with many subprograms, it is often useful to arrange the subprograms in alphabetical order of their names so as to make them easily locatable in the program listing produced by the compiler. It is not necessary to do so, however, and you may well have a more logical arrangement for them. Remember that statement functions are only visible to the subprogram or main program in which they are defined. If you have a statement function that is needed in two different program units, it will need to be defined in both of them. If this occurs across several program units, you may consider it better to rewrite it as a function subprogram.

Fig. 10.1 represents a typical FORTRAN job prepared for input on punched cards. The ordering would be the same for direct input through a terminal input device, such as a visual display unit, but it should be emphasised that the precise details may vary from computer system to computer system and should be checked in the system reference manual.

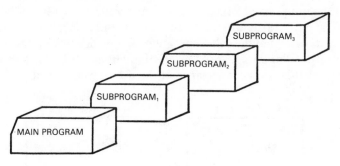

**Fig. 10.1**

## The COMMON statement

In the examples of subprograms given so far, the transfer of information between the calling program and the subprogram has been explicit, in that there has usually been an argument list. The idea of *common storage* – that is, an area of memory common to both the called and the calling program unit – was introduced so that this transfer of information could be effected in an implicit and efficient manner. Its use means that argument lists can, in certain circumstances, be dispensed with, and the overall result is usually a more efficient program in terms of both storage used and execution time. However, care is needed if programs are to remain easy to understand by the reader, and there is an anti-common lobby which believes that the argument list leaves no room for doubt or error. I shall detail the important relevant facts and leave you to choose for yourself.

When a program and its associated subprograms are executed, it is usual for both the main program and its subprograms to be held in the machine's main memory at the same time. This may not be possible in the case of very large jobs, but we shall consider the more usual situation. The main program occupies one part of

memory, and the subprograms will each be held in separate sections
of memory. Each program unit will have its own memory area for
holding the variables and constants to which it needs to refer. The
situation is illustrated in Fig. 10.2(a).

An alternative to this is, while still allowing the main program
and subprograms to occupy areas of memory, to assign the variables
– or at any rate some of them – to a set of memory locations in such a
way that those of the calling program occupy the same places as the
corresponding variables of the called subprogram. This is shown in
Fig. 10.2(b) and is an instance of the use of common storage.

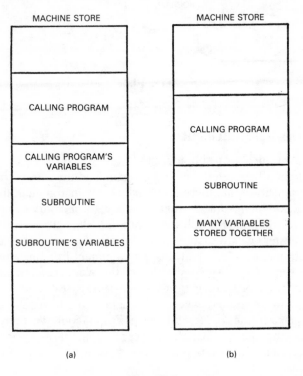

Fig. 10.2

It will be apparent that if two variables are both allocated to the
same memory location in this common storage area, their values at
any given instant will be identical. It follows that any changes of

value that occur in the subprogram will be propagated automatically into the calling program, and vice versa.

Variables are placed into common storage by using the COMMON statement. The following example shows the statements needed to ensure that the arrays CATS and ANIMLS, each with 30 elements, defined in different program units, share the same memory space.

In the calling program:

```
DIMENSION CATS(30)
COMMON CATS
```

In the called program:

```
DIMENSION ANIMLS(30)
COMMON ANIMLS
```

In just the same way as dimension information can be incorporated into a type statement, it can be given in a COMMON statement. We thus get economy of effort with no loss of readability, and might have written, in the calling program:

```
COMMON CATS(30)
```

and in the called program:

```
COMMON ANIMLS(30)
```

Whichever way it is done, the effect is to ensure that the names CATS, in the first program unit, and ANIMLS, in the second, refer to the same set of 30 memory locations. Any alteration in value of an element of CATS results in a similar change in the value of the corresponding element of ANIMLS. There is thus no need for the name of either array to appear in an argument list. Indeed, it is not permissible to use a variable name as a dummy argument if it appears in a COMMON statement of the same subprogram.

Exactly the same mechanics may be used for placing simple variables into common storage, and any number of variables may appear in a COMMON statement. The important point is that common storage is allocated on a first-come, first-served basis; the variables at corresponding positions in two COMMON statements in different program units will be allocated to the same memory location. For instance, in the calling program,

```
COMMON X, Y, Z(120), P(32), Q
```

has the effect of reserving the next 155 REAL storage locations in the common area for X, Y, Z, P and Q. In the called program, we might have

```
COMMON A, B, C(120), D(32), E
```

which will assign A, B, C, D and E to the same storage locations.

Yet another subprogram might be interested only in the fifth variable in the common area, that called Q in the first program and E in the second. The following COMMON statement would make it available by, in effect, 'skipping over' the irrelevant names:

```
COMMON DUMMY(154), R
```

It was not necessary to use the particular name 'DUMMY', but it does indicate that that particular array is of no special interest, and that the last variable in common is the one we shall be using (by yet another name).

## Named COMMON blocks

Common variables declared in the way just discussed are available to any subprogram that includes a similar COMMON statement. However, for convenience, it is often preferable to give another program unit access only to a subset of the variables held in common storage, and to make different subsets available to different program units. This can be done by allocating the different subsets to different *named blocks* of common storage. You will realise, of course, that no variable can appear in more than one block of common storage. This is a particularly useful feature in FORTRAN 77 (though it was available for its predecessors) because the nature of character variables is such that they need to be stored separately from numeric variables. One result of this is that character variables may not appear in the same common block as variables of any other type; without the named COMMON feature, we could put character variables, or numeric variables, into a block of common storage, but not both. If we use separate named blocks of memory, however, we can accommodate both in common storage.

A common block is named by having that name appear in a COMMON statement between two slashes, thus:

```
COMMON /CHARS/ LTRS(26), DGTS(10), REST(18)
COMMON /NUMS/ ALPHA, BETA, X(250), Y, Z
```

These two common blocks, called CHARS and NUMS, respectively, will be allocated separate areas of memory. As many different blocks may be named as are needed. In another program unit,

```
COMMON /CHARS/ A(26), N(10), OTHERS(18)
```

would make the variables of CHARS accessible, but those of NUMS would remain invisible.

Variables of LOGICAL type may share common storage with numeric variables, but not with CHARACTER variables.

It is not necessary (though some would consider it desirable) to use a different COMMON statement for each block of common storage that is declared. Several blocks may be declared in a single statement:

```
COMMON /CHARS/ L(26), N(10), R(18) /NUMS/ A, B,
C(250), P, Q
```

You have the option, if you feel strongly about it, of placing a comma before the name of the second and subsequent common blocks.

The programmer has considerable freedom in the way in which he lays out his COMMON declarations. When the program is compiled, allocation of common is an accumulative process, each block being treated as a separate entity. One un-named block is permitted, declared in the manner shown when the topic was first introduced. This is often referred to as 'blank' common, because its 'name' is an empty string, sometimes written – when it is important to make the distinction – as '/ /'.

The accumulative allocation of common storage means that there may be several COMMON statements in one program unit, all naming the same common block. All that happens is that the compiler appends each set of variables to the appropriate block as, and in the order that, they are encountered. The following have the same overall effect:

```
(a) COMMON A, B, C
    COMMON /FRED/ D(10), E
    COMMON /PETER/ F, G,H(5) // P, Q
    COMMON /PETER/ R(2), S, T
    COMMON /FRED/ U /PETER/ V // W, X, Y(12)
    COMMON /PETER/ Z
(b) COMMON A, B, C, P, Q, W, X, Y(12)
    COMMON /FRED/ D(10), E, U
    COMMON /PETER/ F, G, H(5), R(2), S, T, V, Z
```

An interesting feature of the use of common storage between subprograms is that, since the subprograms are compiled separately, different routines may choose to interpret the common areas in different ways. This needs great care in its use, and if items of one type in routine A are interpreted as though they were of a different type in routine B (for instance, routine A may specify a set of real values and routine B choose to treat the same storage area as a set of integers) one will very often need to have a detailed understanding of how these data types are represented on the machine you are using. Since this varies from machine to machine, such juggling should be avoided if you are trying to write programs of general utility. It should probably be avoided anyway! Here is a simple example in which an array is treated differently in two subprograms:

```
      SUBROUTINE INPUT           SUBROUTINE SUM(V)
      COMMON X(10, 10)           COMMON Q(100)
      ...                        V = 0.0
      DO 30 I=1,10               DO 10 I=1,100
        DO 20 J=1,10               V = V + Q(I)
          READ *, X(I,J)    10  CONTINUE
   20   CONTINUE                END
   30 CONTINUE
      CALL SUM(S)
      ...
```

No real problem arises here. COMMON $X(10,10)$ reserves 100 memory locations for REAL type variables in blank common. COMMON $Q(100)$ refers to the same 100 locations – the first 100 in the blank common area – and gives them the name of a REAL array, Q. The different treatment lies in the fact that X is a two-dimensional array, Q is one-dimensional. When execution speed is very important, such an approach may be justifiable on the grounds that it is quicker to handle singly-subscripted variables than it is to deal with those having two or more. Again, it is a piece of program trickery that is probably best avoided except in very special circumstances.

## The EQUIVALENCE statement

The effect of the COMMON statement is to allow a number of program units to communicate with one another by means of variables held in a commonly accessible storage area. Each subprogram may refer to the variables in the common area by whatever names happen to be most suitable within that routine. This will often – though not invariably – mean that a variable in a particular memory location is known by different names in different subprograms.

There are occasions when it is useful to be able to refer to a storage location by two, or even more, names *in the same program unit*. If, for instance, a program refers to two variables, A and B, but these two variables are never in active use at the same time then, if there is reason to conserve the use of memory, it may seem reasonable to allow them to occupy the same memory location. The principle is the same as might have been applied on the troop ship 'QUEEN MARY' during the Second World War, when it is said that the beds never got cold because as one man left to go on duty, another came off duty and rolled into it. The statement used in FORTRAN to achieve this would be

```
EQUIVALENCE (A, B)
```

which states that A and B are to share the same storage. They are said to have been *equivalenced* to each other: a reference to A is equivalent to a reference to B. The names could be freely – even randomly – interchanged without changing the effect of the program (though its maintenance might thereby be made rather a problem).

The general form of an EQUIVALENCE statement is

EQUIVALENCE ( list$_1$), (list$_2$), . . . (list$_n$)

in which each list is of the form $v_1, v_2, v_3, . . . v_m$ and the $v$s are either variable names or the names of array elements. Each of the variables in a given list is equivalenced to all the others in the same list.

Since arrays are stored sequentially in memory, it follows that the equivalencing of one element from each of two arrays has the effect of equivalencing a number, or even all, of the arrays' elements. Thus, given the statements

```
DIMENSION X(20), Y(20)
EQUIVALENCE (X(1), Y(1))
```

it is obvious that the whole of array Y must be equivalenced to the corresponding elements of array X. A reference to x(5) gets the same data item as would a reference to Y(5). But suppose one of the arrays is two-dimensional?

```
DIMENSION A(2, 5), B(10)
EQUIVALENCE (A(1, 1), B(1))
```

If we refer to B(6), for example, to which element of A will it be equivalenced? It may be important that we should know this; here is a rule that will enable us to work it out: *FORTRAN arrays are stored in such a way that the right-most subscript varies most rapidly and the left-most subscript is the slowest to change.* In the case of a two-dimensional array, this is equivalent to saying that the array is stored a column at a time. The idea takes a little getting used to, but FORTRAN programmers have long since learned to live with it. Our array A will thus be allocated to 10 sequential memory locations, by the compiler, with its elements stored in the order

$$A_{1,1} \quad A_{2,1} \quad A_{1,2} \quad A_{2,2} \quad A_{1,3} \quad A_{2,3} \quad A_{1,4} \quad A_{2,4} \quad A_{1,5} \quad A_{2,5}$$

The elements of B, of course, are stored in their natural order:

$$B_1 \quad B_2 \quad B_3 \quad B_4 \quad B_5 \quad B_6 \quad B_7 \quad B_8 \quad B_9 \quad B_{10}$$

It follows that B(6) would be equivalenced to A(2, 3).

The EQUIVALENCE statement originated from the days when machines had small memories and programmers needed an intimate knowledge of the inner workings of the machine. It is a feature rarely likely to be needed when using a modern mainframe computer. Bear in mind the important distinction between COMMON and EQUIVALENCE:

1 COMMON is used for sharing storage between *different program units*.

2 EQUIVALENCE is for sharing storage within *a single program unit*.

Its use is not restricted to arrays; single variables can be equivalenced to one another. It is recommended that any given equivalence be between entities of the same type. Character items may only be equivalenced to other character items.

## Interaction of COMMON and EQUIVALENCE statements

Despite their different applications, it often happens that a data item is equivalenced to another one that is in common storage. It would be invalid to equivalence two items that were *both* in common storage since, within a program unit, every item declared in a COMMON statement must be allocated its own memory space. Equivalencing such items thus makes no sense.

When a variable is equivalenced to one that is already in a common area, that variable is itself – as you might expect, since it shares the same memory locations – brought into common storage. It is quite possible that a side effect of such an equivalence could be to increase the size of the common area, a sneaky effect which the following example will illustrate.

```
COMMON X(10)
DIMENSION Y(10)
EQUIVALENCE (X(3), Y(1))
```

The result of compiling this sequence is to bring *the whole of the array* Y into common. A consideration of the COMMON statement alone would not indicate that any such thing was intended, so if you do something like this, it would be as well to include an explanatory comment to help the poor maintenance programmer at some unspecified future date. Fig. 10.3(a) shows the situation. In this case, the common area is being extended in a direction away from its origin, and such extension is permissible. Now look at this one:

```
COMMON X(10)
DIMENSION Y(10)
EQUIVALENCE (X(3), Y(4))
```

Despite its very similar appearance to that of the previous example, this sequence is quite unacceptable. If it were possible to achieve this equivalence, the bringing of the array Y into the common area would involve the extension of that area backwards beyond x(1). Such backward extension is forbidden (see Fig. 10.3(b)).

To finish this chapter, here are two complete examples of subroutine and function respectively, each with the main program that invokes it. The first is a subroutine that sorts the first N values of the array x into ascending numerical order. The routine has no argument list, since the arguments are transferred through the common storage area. The associated main program reads values into the array, calls SORT to sort them, and then prints the median (i.e. central) value.

```
PROGRAM MIDDLE
COMMON A(1000), N
```

```
C        READ THE ARRAY SIZE. MAXIMUM SIZE IS 1000.
C        WE SHOULD CHECK, BUT DON'T IN THIS EXAMPLE.
         READ *, N
C        ... AND NOW THE ARRAY
         DO 10 I = 1, N
         READ *, A(I)
   10 CONTINUE
C        SORT THE ARRAY
         CALL SORT
C        FIND THE MEDIAN — USE THE VALUE AT OR
C        JUST BELOW N/2
         AMED = A(N/2)
         PRINT *, 'THE MEDIAN VALUE IS ', AMED
         END
         SUBROUTINE SORT
         COMMON X(1000), NX
C        ONLY THE NAMES HAVE CHANGED. THE SAME
C        MEMORY CELLS AS A AND N (MAIN PROGRAM)
C        ARE USED
         DO 20 I = 1, NX — 1
C        AT EACH RETURN TO THIS POINT, ALL THE ELEMENTS
C        OF X BEFORE X(I) ARE IN ORDER
         DO 10 J = I + 1, NX
C        J IS THE STARTING POINT (IN X) FOR THE NEXT
C        SCAN. WHEN J = NX THE SORT IS FINISHED
         IF (X(I) .GT. X(J)) THEN
C        EXCHANGE
           TEMP = X(I)
           X(I) = X(J)
           X(J) = TEMP
         END IF
   10    CONTINUE
   20 CONTINUE
C        THE ARRAY IS NOW SORTED
         END
```

The sorting algorithm is summarised in the flowchart of Fig. 10.4. On the first scan through the array, the smallest element is located and exchanged with that in the first position. Scanning then starts again at the second position, and the process is repeated. Each scan involves the examination of one element fewer than the previous scan, until only two remain. When these have been arranged in order, the sort is complete. Do not be misled into thinking that this is a particularly efficient sorting method – but it serves our present purpose.

Remember that when a SUBROUTINE subprogram has no arguments, there is no need to write the parentheses that are *required* for a FUNCTION subprogram.

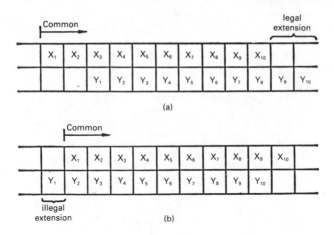

**Fig. 10.3**

The final example is a LOGICAL FUNCTION subprogram to check the validity, or otherwise, of an international standard book number (ISBN). For ease of reference, every book published in a number of countries, including Britain and the USA, is given a unique identifying number called its ISBN. It will usually be found at the front of the book, with the date of publication, printer's credits, etc.

The ISBN consists of 10 digits, or nine digits and a letter. The letter, when it appears, is invariably 'x'. The first nine digits form a code which identifies the publisher and the book. The last character is a check on the correctness of those nine digits. So if you were to order a book, quoting the ISBN, and you copied it down wrongly, the function given here would be able to detect that the number contained an error and appropriate action could be taken.

The way in which the check is performed is this:

1 Each digit is considered to have an associated 'weight'. These weights are, from right to left, the values in the sequence 1, 2, 3, ..., 9, 10.
2 Each digit is multiplied by its weight, and the products are added together.
3 The final sum is divided by 11.
4 If there is no remainder after the division, the ISBN is correct. Any remainder at all implies an error somewhere in the ISBN.

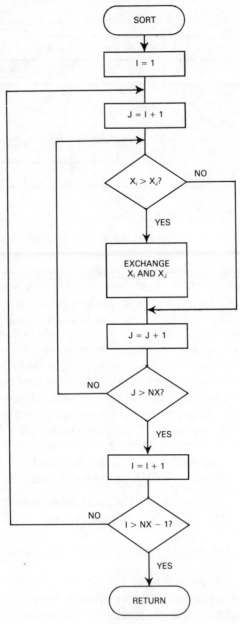

**Fig. 10.4**

The right-most 'check digit' is calculated by a similar process (in reverse) when the first nine digits are allocated at publication. A check digit of 'x' is intended to represent the value 10.

The following ISBNs are valid: 0 07 015564 X and 0 340 19495 2 (the character groupings may be ignored). These are invalid: 0 102 05499 X and 0 07 034955 5. Check them for yourself.

(The numbers in the left-hand margin are for reference in the commentary which follows the program.)

```
          PROGRAM ISBNCH
1         LOGICAL CHECK
2         CHARACTER * 10 BOOK

   C      THIS PROGRAM READS IN EACH ISBN AS A STRING
   C      OF TEN CHARACTERS, AND CALLS CHECK TO
   C      DETERMINE WHETHER THEY CONSTITUTE A VALID
   C      ISBN. THE PROGRAM IS TERMINATED BY AN
   C      INPUT WHOSE FIRST CHARACTER IS AN ASTERISK.

3      10 READ *, BOOK
4         IF (BOOK(1:1) .EQ. '*') STOP
5         IF (CHECK(BOOK)) THEN
            PRINT *, BOOK, ' IS O.K.'
          ELSE
            PRINT *, BOOK, ' DOES NOT CHECK.'
          END IF
6         GO TO 10
7         END

          FUNCTION CHECK(ISBN)
8         LOGICAL CHECK
9         CHARACTER * 10 ISBN
          CHARACTER CH
10        INTEGER SUM, WEIGHT, VAL
          LOGICAL DIGIT, FINALX
11        CHARACTER. X
12
13        DIGIT(X) = '0' .LE. X .AND. X .LE. '9'
14        FINAL(X) = X .EQ. 'X' .AND. I .EQ. 10
15        VAL(X) = ICHAR(X) — ICHAR('0')
16        SUM = 0
          DO 10 I=1,10
17          WEIGHT = 11 — I
            CH = ISBN(I:I)
18          IF (DIGIT(CH)) THEN
19            SUM = SUM + VAL(CH)*WEIGHT
20          ELSE IF FINALX(CH) THEN
21            SUM = SUM + 10
            ELSE
```

```
22          CHECK = .FALSE.
            RETURN
         END IF
   10 CONTINUE
23      CHECK = MOD(SUM, 11) .EQ. 0
        END
```

## Commentary

1 The external functions used must have their types declared if they do not conform to the INTEGER/REAL naming convention.

2 BOOK is the name of the 10-character variable used to contain the ISBN.

3 We shall return to this point, hence the statement number 10. Remember to enclose the data string in single quotes when it is input as a character string using 'READ *'.

4 BOOK(1:1) is the substring of BOOK consisting of the single character in the first position of the string.

5 This is a reference to the function CHECK, which returns the LOGICAL value, .TRUE. or .FALSE., depending on whether the ISBN is valid or not.

6 This closes the loop.

7 Every program unit must have END as its last statement. Only one END per unit.

8 A function whose name does not conform to the INTEGER/REAL naming convention must contain a declaration of its type. In this case, it could equally well have been contained in the FUNCTION statement, which would then have been LOGICAL FUNCTION CHECK(ISBN); if we had done this, the statement LOGICAL CHECK could have been omitted.

9 We have been rather rigid here. The ISBN string must contain exactly 10 characters. A more general approach would perhaps use CHARACTER* (*) and use the LEN function to determine how many characters are to be processed.

10 VAL is a statement function that returns an INTEGER result. DIGIT and FINALX are statement functions, each returning a LOGICAL result. None of them conform to the name/type convention and so they must be declared.

11 X is a dummy variable, representing a character, used by the statement functions. It needs to be declared, so that it is not

confused with a REAL variable, which would not be allowed the character operations specified.

12 Most FORTRAN systems will ignore blank lines. Their use for improving readability is strongly recommended. If your system does not like blank lines, you will have to make them into comments by putting a 'c' or an '*' in column 1. But *do* use them.

13 We know that FORTRAN requires the digits to occupy 10 consecutive positions in the collating sequence, in the order 0, 1, ..., 8, 9. DIGIT is .TRUE. if x is a character in this range, .FALSE. otherwise.

14 Do not confuse the character 'x' and the dummy character variable x. This statement function returns .TRUE. if we are looking at the last 'digit' and it happens to be the letter x.

15 You will recall that ICHAR produces a unique integer value for each character in the collating sequence. Since '0' through '9' forms an unbroken sequence, so do the corresponding values produced by ICHAR. Hence, ICHAR('0') − ICHAR('0') will produce the value 0, and, at the other extreme, ICHAR('9') − ICHAR('0') will produce the value 9. We convert a numeric *character* into the corresponding numeric *value*, so that we can do arithmetic with it. Obviously, the intermediate numeric characters will also be converted into the appropriate values.

16 We are to calculate a sum of products. It will be developed in the variable SUM, which must be initialised here.

17 We are fortunate in that the set of weights is a simple sequence from 10 down to 1 in steps of 1. This enables us to calculate the weight value from the position of the digit currently being considered. As I varies from 1 to 10, so 11 − I varies from 10 down to 1.

18 Is the character at position I of the string a digit?

19 If so, determine its numerical value, multiply it by the appropriate weight and add it to the sum of products.

20 If not, there is a chance that it is the letter 'x' in the last position of the string. If so, ....

21 ... since 'x' means 10, and the weight is 1, we just add 10 to the sum.

22 The only possibility left is that we have an invalid character in this position. The whole thing is thus invalid. Set CHECK .FALSE., and exit.

23 If the remainder is zero, the right-hand side expression is .TRUE., if not, it is .FALSE. Set CHECK accordingly and exit.

## Exercises

1 A one-dimensional array is called WEEK and has seven elements. Write a subroutine subprogram, with no arguments, which will add together the elements of WEEK, leaving the sum in the variable TAKE.

2 Given a raw mark, $x$, an examiner produces an adjusted mark, $x'$, by applying the formula:

$$x' = ax + b$$

where $a$ and $b$ are suitable adjustment constants.

Write a subroutine subprogram to read in and print a set of raw marks, printing by the side of each its corresponding adjusted mark. Use $-1$ as a sentinel value to mark the end of the list. No other value will be negative.

3 TEXT is an array of 80-character strings. The last element of TEXT has an '*' as its first character.

Write a subroutine to scan TEXT and, by counting question marks, determine how many questions it contains. Add a suitable main program, so that the subroutine can be tested.

4 Write a subroutine that receives as an argument a single character and packs it into the next available position of the CHARACTER array called STRING, which has 20 six-character elements. Assume that STRING is in common storage, together with a NEXT, pointer (i.e. integer variable) that indicates the next free character position in STRING. Initially, NEXT will have been given the value 1; when NEXT exceeds 120, STRING is to be printed and NEXT reset to its initial value.

# 11

# Input and output

So far, we have managed to write programs of varying degrees of complexity using only the most elementary of input and output commands. All input has been assumed to be from the default device – usually the card reader or the VDU keyboard – and it has been assumed that all output would be to the other default device – usually the line printer, or the VDU screen. Further, we have needed only the simplest layouts of results and data. In such circumstances, the very basic READ * and PRINT * commands have been quite adequate. Both of these statements are special forms of the READ and PRINT statements, in which the asterisk means 'Use the predefined standard data and results layout' and the default devices are used because no other is specified.

It is generally necessary to supply the system with *two* different pieces of information when transferring data into or out of the central processor, *plus* a list of the data items to be transferred. These two pieces of information are:

1 The device to or from which the data is being moved.
2 The *format* in which that data is to be found (on input) or laid out (on output).

In this chapter, we shall look at some of the simpler ways in which the transfer of data is effected in FORTRAN.

## The READ statement

The basic form of the READ statement is

READ f, *list*

in which f is either an '*', meaning 'Use the default data format', or a statement number, which identifies a FORMAT statement in which full details of the layout of the data are given. More rarely, f may be a character constant, consisting of a list of *format specifications* which indicate the layout of the data. This list has to be enclosed in parentheses and, of course, being a character constant, further enclosed in quotes. This simple READ has no means of indicating where the data is coming from, so the default device is assumed; *list* is the list of data items to be input.

### Examples

READ *, A, B, I
— We have met this one often before.

READ 10, X, Y, K, Q
— Read values for X, Y, K and Q which will be arranged on the input medium in the manner indicated in statement number 10.

READ '(3I4)', I, J, K
— Read values for I, J and K, each of which is an integer occupying four character positions, one after the other on the same line of the input medium.

Every computer system has, in practice, a number of different input and output devices, each of which has a unique identifying 'code' number by which it is known to the FORTRAN system. Typically, this is 5 for the card reader, 6 for the printer, 1 for both the VDU keyboard and the screen (they can be distinguished by the direction of the data transfer). If one wishes to be quite specific as to which device is to be used, there is an alternative form of the READ statement:

READ($u$, $f$) *list*

Here, *f* is again a format identifier, and *list* names the data items; but the input device (or unit) is specified by the value of *u*. Note the use of parentheses in this alternative form of the READ statement. What is shown here is the normal minimum *control information list*. We shall see later that it can be much more involved.

Here are the same input statements as those given earlier, but expressed in this more general manner. It is assumed that the input device is unit 5.

```
READ(5, *) A, B, I
```
– Note that '\*' still means that the standard formats are to be used.
This is usually called 'free-format input'.

```
READ(5, 10) X, Y, K, Q
```
– The statement numbered '10' contains the format information. This is possibly the commonest form of input statement.

```
READ(5, '(3I4)') I, J, K
```
– An awkward, but often useful, form – best used when the quoted format specification is only used once in the program unit.

It must be emphasised at this point that there is no universal standard set of device codes by which input and output units are designated. The values given in these examples are chosen because one often finds them used, but it is essential to check with the appropriate manual for the computer system you are using before you attempt to run your programs.

## The input/output list

The READ statement indicates, by means of the list of names that appears in it, *what* is to be read in, and the order in which data items are to be allocated to the named variables. It also specifies *where* these data items are coming from (the input device) and, as we shall see later, *what to do* if certain problems arise – such as running out of data. The associated FORMAT statement indicates *how* the data items are to be found on the input medium and how they are to be interpreted (as REAL, INTEGER or LOGICAL values, for example).

The list can be much more complicated than we have seen so far. It is composed of a number of *list elements*, of which the simple variable is one example. Subscripted variables may also be used, and the type of a list element may be any of those available in FORTRAN 77, some of which we have not yet considered: REAL, INTEGER, CHARACTER, LOGICAL, DOUBLE PRECISION and COMPLEX. This list should not contain any constant values – it would scarcely make sense to attempt to assign a new value to a constant.

The amount of information transferred into memory by a single READ statement is variable, but it is never less than one *physical record*. This is what is contained in one punched card, or on one line input from the VDU keyboard; when other devices, such as magnetic tape or discs are used, a physical record can often be quite large. How much of this physical record is used to hold data is a matter to be decided by the programmer, but he *must* know, or else he will be unable to write the correct FORMAT statements. FORTRAN also gives the programmer the ability to specify that more than one record is read (or written). This will be explained in the section on the FORMAT statement. It will very often happen, however, that the terms 'card' (or 'line') and 'record' are synonymous.

The input of a few simple variables is a straightforward business, and we have seen a number of examples already. Arrays, though, may present a problem. Suppose, for example, that we have to read values from cards into the first 15 elements of the 30-element array Q. How could this be achieved?

One possibility would be to write a very long statement:

```
READ(5, 200) Q(1), Q(2), Q(3), ... , Q(14), Q(15)
```

This would be tedious for the programmer, and somewhat lacking in style, but it would work. It is a good thing, however, that we are not reading 500 values into a larger array!

Another approach would be to use a DO loop:

```
      DO 10 I=1, 15
        READ(5, 200) Q(I)
   10 CONTINUE
```

but, since each READ reads from at least one card, this would be a little wasteful of resources (though economical in terms of programming effort), because only one value would be read from each card.

If we make the assumption that there is room on one card for five values, the two approaches can be combined:

```
DO 10 I=1, 11, 5
   READ(5, 200) Q(I),Q(I+1),Q(I+2),Q(I+3),Q(I+4)
10 CONTINUE
```

Again, this would work and is perhaps the best solution so far. But there is an alternative: the *implied* DO construction. This sets up a structure very similar to that of a DO loop, but without the word 'DO'. It may be used only for certain types of list, including those for input and output statements. For our example, the implied DO would make it look like this:

```
READ(5, 200) (Q(I), I=1, 15)
```

In words, this means: 'Read, from device 5 and in accordance with the layout specified in FORMAT statement 200, values of Q(I) for values of I from 1 to 15, inclusive.'

The effect of this statement is precisely the same as that of the first example. All 15 elements are read as a single *logical record* – a related collection of data items – though they may have been contained in several physical records. As with the standard DO loop, the increment may be varied, and the trip count is calculated in exactly the same way.

```
READ(1,300) (NAME(I), I=1, M, 2)
```

In this case, of course, it is important to ensure that M has been assigned a value before an attempt is made to execute the READ statement.

Implied DO constructions may be mixed with ordinary variables in the list of a READ statement:

```
READ(5, 3002) X, Y, (A(J), J=1, 20), L, M, N
```

This will have the effect of reading X, then Y, then 20 values for the first 20 elements of the array A, followed by L, M and N.

In the next example, one of the implied DO parameters is read in during the execution of the statement that contains the implied DO:

```
READ(5, 355) N, (X(I), I=1, N)
```

The value of N is read, followed by values for the first N elements of the array x. When this technique is used, it is obviously important that N should be at a position in the list that precedes its use as a parameter of the implied DO.

Nested implied DO constructions can be quite useful:

```
READ(2, 333) ((FLOW(J, K), K=1, 4), J=1, 3)
```

The parentheses show the nesting structure: K will be varied from 1 to 4 while the value of J is 1; then J will be increased to 2, and K will again take the values 1 to 4; finally, J's value becomes 3 and again K's values are varied from 1 to 4. This is roughly equivalent to the following nested DO loop, except that all the values are read (using the implied DO) as a single logical record:

```
      DO 10 J=1, 3
         DO 5 K=1, 4
            READ(2, 334) FLOW(J, K)
 5       CONTINUE
10    CONTINUE
```

A different format label has been used deliberately, since the layout will have to be one array element per line.

## Input of complete arrays

One often needs to assign values to every element of an array, rather than – as in the examples given above – to parts of it. Given a 20-element, one-dimensional array VALUES, there are a number of ways in which every element could have a value read into it. One of the simplest would be:

```
READ(2, 111) (VALUES(I), I=1, 20)
```

and this is probably the best approach, since there is no possibility of ambiguity and every element is named in the order in which it will be used.

There is another construction frequently used, in which only the *name* of the array appears in the list of the READ statement:

```
READ(2, 111) VALUES
```

would have exactly the same effect as the previous example. One disadvantage of this method is that it does not make explicit how many items are to be read, nor the order in which the values are allocated. As far as the compiler is concerned, it will be aware, from the previous DIMENSION statement, that VALUES is an array and that it has 20 elements. It then has the relatively simple task of generating machine instructions that will fill all 20 elements with values from the specified input device, in the order VALUES(1), VALUES(2), . . . VALUES(20).

Note that this approach is only usable when *the whole array* is to be processed. If only a part of the array is to be processed, then the elements concerned must be named explicitly, using one of the methods described earlier. The method may be used with two- and higher-dimensioned arrays, but in such cases it is important to be aware of the order in which FORTRAN 77 requires that array elements should be assigned, in the absence of specific information; this default is *column order*, and we have already seen one example of this in the section on the EQUIVALENCE statement. Just to remind you, consider the array MATRIX:

```
DIMENSION MATRIX(3, 3)
```

MATRIX has three rows and three columns. If we now execute the statement

```
READ(5, 100) MATRIX
```

the values will be read in the order MATRIX(1, 1), MATRIX(2, 1), MATRIX(3, 1), MATRIX(1, 2), MATRIX(2, 2), MATRIX(3, 2), MATRIX(1, 3), MATRIX(2, 3) and MATRIX(3, 3).

Note that the left-most subscript is varying the most rapidly. The principle extends to three- and higher-dimensioned arrays: the further to the left a subscript is, the faster it changes. Obviously it is most important to bear in mind this ordering, and ensure that the data items are presented to the input device in the expected order.

## Testing for the end of file

The records constituting the set of data being processed are said to form a *file* of data. When all the data records have been read in, we say that the end of the data file (or, more usually, the 'end of file') has been reached. The early examples of data processing involved the use of a sentinel data value to mark the end of file, and a special test for that particular value had to be written into the program.

This can often be inconvenient, because there may not be a data value that is so unusual that it is unlikely to turn up as a normal data item. It is much more convenient to be able to say, in effect, 'If there is any data left, read the next record; otherwise, branch to the statement labelled (for example) 9999.' This can be achieved by making an addition to the control information list of the READ statement:

```
READ(5, 1000, END = 9999) P, Q, K
```

This statement attempts to read values from unit 5, in accordance with the format specified in statement 1000, but if the end of file has been reached, a branch to the instruction labelled 9999 is made instead.

It is quite usual to write input statements in this form. One can, however, be much more specific, and expand the control information list, like this:

```
READ(UNIT=5, FMT=1000, END=9999) P, Q, K
```

When these 'keywords' are used, their order of appearance is no longer important; this would have the same effect:

```
READ(END=9999,UNIT=5,FMT=1000) P, Q, K
```

It is better to be consistent, though, and the simple form is probably best for most purposes.

## Error conditions

Another control information list item is used to enable the programmer to retain control if an error condition arises during an input or output operation. It causes a branch to the indicated statement number if an error condition occurs.

```
READ(5, 1000, END=9999, ERR=9998) P, Q, K
```

An error in reading will cause a branch to the instruction labelled 9998. More information can be obtained as to the cause of the error by assigning a variable to receive a code if an error occurs. This can then be examined or displayed by the program and may be of help in pin-pointing the source of the error. The actual value of the code will be specified in the manual for the computer installation you are using, but the assignment of a variable to receive it is quite straightforward:

```
READ(5, 1000, END=9999, ERR=9998, IOSTAT=ERRCDE)
*    P, Q, K
```

(It is assumed that ERRCDE has previously been declared as an integer.) In this case, if either end of file or an error condition arises, the appropriate code will be placed into ERRCDE, and the specified branch will occur.

It is not uncommon for programs to be written that contain no such error traps. If anything goes wrong in such a program, what usually happens is that the program is terminated, and the programmer has little idea of what caused the problem except what he may glean from an often cryptic operating system message. It is much better to include these tests and generate one's own meaningful messages.

## The WRITE statement

Much of what has been said about the READ statement applies also to the WRITE statement. It has virtually the same basic structure:

```
WRITE(6, 250) A, B(8), (C(I), I=1, 7)
```

will send the values of A, the eighth element of B and the first seven elements of C to device number 6 – probably the line printer. All this will be in accordance with the FORMAT statement labelled 250.

The number of characters output on a line depends on the device you are using: line printers usually print 132, or perhaps 120, characters per line; teletype (teletypewriter) devices only about 72; VDU screens allow for up to 80 characters per line, depending on the manufacturer. The characters may be any of those in the FORTRAN character set, and many systems allow other, non-FORTRAN, characters to be output as well.

A WRITE statement is not *required* to have a list of variables. Sometimes it is more convenient not to have one, giving a statement which looks like this:

```
WRITE(6, 540)
```

This may be useful for printing headings, for instance, in which predefined text is to be output, but no computed values are involved. So we can treat the WRITE statement in exactly the same way as the READ statement. The data transfer is in the opposite direction, of course! The ability to output arrays using the implied DO feature applies equally to writing, and complete arrays may be output (in column order) by supplying the name only.

## The remaining data types

We have already considered the most important types of FORTRAN data: REAL, INTEGER, LOGICAL and CHARACTER. Sometimes it happens that the precision (number of significant figures used in calculation) of REAL values is insufficient to give the required accuracy in the results. If that is the case, it is possible to increase that precision so that the number of significant figures is approximately doubled. This is particularly useful when, in long calculations, rounding errors are beginning to accumulate, giving answers that are unreliable. If the affected variables are declared as being of type DOUBLE PRECISION, the onset of such inaccuracies can be considerably delayed. The reason that errors occur is that the floating-point representation of real numbers is only approximate, but the more digits we have in the mantissa, the more accurate the approximation becomes. Since integers can be represented exactly, there is no need for double-precision integers, generally speaking. One slight disadvantage of using double-precision is that the speed of computation is usually quite markedly reduced. Double-precision constants are written in a form similar to that used for real constants (the exponent form), but using the letter D rather than E to separate the exponent. Thus, the number $0.2135476897645 \times 10^7$ would be written as 0.2135476897645D7.

Some users find it convenient to have a facility for handling complex numbers directly. To meet their needs, FORTRAN offers a specific COMPLEX type, each COMPLEX item being composed of two REAL items, one for the real part and one for the imaginary part of the complex value represented. Many intrinsic functions are available to manipulate COMPLEX quantities. We shall pay very little attention to this rather specialised data type, however: those interested are referred to larger volumes and the FORTRAN 77 standard documentation.

## FORMAT specification

The job of the FORMAT statement is to ensure that, on input, the FORTRAN system knows how to interpret the character string which it 'sees' – as REAL, DOUBLE PRECISION, INTEGER, CHARACTER or LOGICAL items. On output, the same information is required, plus the details of spacing between values, number of decimal places needed, whether the normal or the scientific (exponent) form of real numbers is wanted, and so on. All this information is given in the *field specifications* in the FORMAT statement.

The general form of the FORMAT statement is as follows:

*xxx* FORMAT (*list of format specifications*)

where *xxx* is the statement number that uniquely identifies this FORMAT statement; it is this value that is used in the associated READ or WRITE statements. FORTRAN 77 offers the user a wide variety of format specifications, which are described in more detail in the following sections.

## The I specification

This is used when the data being transferred is of INTEGER type. Here is a simple example:

```
      READ(5, 100) MAN
  100 FORMAT(I5)
```

This is interpreted as: 'Read a record from device number 5 (this will often be the card reader). The first *five* characters of the record are to be interpreted as an *integer*, and that integer value is to be stored in the variable called MAN.' An alternative way of writing the same instruction, useful if the same format is not to be used elsewhere in the program unit, is to include the format specification in the READ (or WRITE) control information list, as we saw at the beginning of this chapter:

```
  READ(5, '(I5)') MAN
```

If several integers are to be input and they are all the same size, we can use a format specification such as this:

```
      READ(5, 25) A, B, C, D, E
   25 FORMAT(5I6)
```

(Presumably, A, ..., E have previously been declared to be integers.) Here it is specified that the input record consists of *five integers*, each of field width *six* characters (i.e. each one is six characters long, and they appear on the record one after the other, five values in all). A typical input record for this statement would be the following, in which you will note that each number has its units digit in the right-most position of its 'field' (the part of the record it occupies).

123456234567345678456789567890
‾‾‾‾‾‾ ‾‾‾‾‾‾ ‾‾‾‾‾‾ ‾‾‾‾‾‾ ‾‾‾‾‾‾
  A      B      C      D     E

Here is another, in which the values are more easily separated, since they are not using their total field widths. Nevertheless, the units digit must appear in the correct position in each case, or the wrong value will be read.

  12345  2345   345 45678     5
  ‾‾‾‾‾ ‾‾‾‾‾ ‾‾‾‾‾ ‾‾‾‾‾ ‾‾‾‾‾
   A     B    C    D     E

Note that spaces are usually interpreted as zeros.

When performing an output operation, the I format specification indicates that the value output is to be regarded as an integer, and it also specifies exactly how much space is to be allowed for it on the output line or record, as we shall see.

## Spacing

In the first example considered above, it was assumed that the data field – five characters in width – started in the first column of the input record. We should also think about how we might handle the situation if the data field were in, for example, columns 11 to 15, with columns 1 to 10 empty (or, at least, of no interest).

What is needed is some means of telling the computer to skip over those first 10 columns, looking only at the succeeding data. FORTRAN 77 offers two ways of doing this: here are the two possible approaches, in their simplest forms.

```
100  FORMAT(10X, I5)
```

Here, '10x' means 'skip over the next 10 columns'. Since this is the first field specification, in this case the 'next' 10 columns happen to be the first 10 columns of the input record. Hence, the data field is taken to be that immediately after the field skipped, i.e. columns 11 to 15, inclusive.

The alternative is this:

```
100 FORMAT(T11, I5)
```

in which 'T' means 'tab' – move to column number given (in this case, 11). Notice that the number after 'T' is the number of the column at which the input or output process is to continue. If one wanted to start at column 13, the field specification would be 12X, or T13, meaning either 'skip the next 12 columns' or 'tab to column 13', respectively. The end result is the same.

Both spacing methods are more frequently used for output results, as in the following example:

```
      WRITE(1, 333) I, J, K
333 FORMAT(10X, I3, 12X, I4, 5X, I5)
```

or, possibly, (the reason for the '1x' is given later):

```
333 FORMAT(1X, T10, I3, T25, I4, T34, I5)
```

The second form is less likely to be used, because it will involve careful column counting to determine the precise number of the column in which each field is to start, whereas if one uses the 'x' field specification, one is more concerned with field *separations*. However, there is a variation of the 'tab' feature that allows it to be used in a relative manner exactly equivalent to the 'x' method. TR$n$, where $n$ represents a positive integer, has the same effect as '$n$x'. 'TR' means 'tab right'. As a matter of interest, there is a corresponding 'TL' (tab left) specification. Using this, with 'TR' and 'x', we could do silly things like

```
      WRITE(1, 334) K, I, J
334 FORMAT(35X, I5, TL30, I3, TR12, I4)
```

Don't! Keep it simple – one day you may have to work out what your program is doing, and why.

In this example, if I = 45, J = 2357 and K = −63, the output should be

- - - - - - - - - - 45 - - - - - - - - - - - - 2357 - - - - - - - - −63

To show the spacing clearly, dashes have been used to represent spaces. They would not, of course, be printed.

If you were to count the number of spaces printed as a result of the '10x' field specification in the last-but-one example, you might be surprised to find that only *nine* spaces had been printed. The one immediately preceding the '45' is part of the three-character field for the variable 'I'. What happened to the tenth space? It will be found that 12x has produced 12 spaces, and 5x has produced five spaces. Only the first field seems to have come out wrongly.

This is quite normal in FORTRAN systems. The information to be printed is collected together and sent to the printer as a string of characters for each line. But the printer also needs to know which line it should print these characters on. Is it the next? Or the next but one? The same one as last time? On a new page? It gets this information by the simple expedient of peeling off the first character of each line, interpreting it as a line-spacing instruction, and then discarding it! It is not printed: it is simply used as a *carriage-control character*.*

In practice, there are only three carriage-control characters worth bothering about. These are the characters zero, one and blank, which have the following effects *before* the line is printed:

| *Control character* | *Effect on printer* |
|---|---|
| 0 | Skip one line |
| blank | Print on the next line |
| 1 | Start a new page |
| + | Print on the same line again |

The last ('+') is included for completeness, but is not often used. See your system reference manual.

**Examples**

(a) To output a heading in the centre of the top line of a new page. The printer has a carriage 120 characters wide.

```
      . . .
      WRITE (6, 1000)
 1000 FORMAT ('1', T51, 'AREA_SALES_REPORT')
      . . .
```

The '1' is used to select the new page.

---

* This does not usually apply when the output is sent to the screen of a visual display unit, for which there are often special control characters.

(b) We have two 1000-element arrays, L and M. It is required to output a table of their corresponding values, double spaced, 25 lines per page, each page numbered in the top right-hand corner.

```
      ...
      INTEGER PAGE
      ...
      DO 20 PAGE = 1, 40
        WRITE (6, 100) PAGE
100     FORMAT ('1', T110, 'PAGE:', I5)
        K = 25 * (PAGE - 1)
        DO 10 LINE = 1, 25
          I = K + LINE
C         THIS SELECTS THE CORRECT ARRAY ELEMENTS
          WRITE (6, 200) L(I), M(I)
200       FORMAT ('0', 10X, I4, 10X, I4)
10      CONTINUE
20    CONTINUE
      ...
```

Individual computer systems may offer extra facilities, but these should be viewed with suspicion and treated with care: almost certainly they are non-standard, and their use will mean problems at a later stage if you wish to run your programs on a different manufacturer's computer.

Returning to the 'x' specification for input, can you see anything wrong with the following FORMAT statement, used to read from a punched card?

```
100 FORMAT (77X, I5)
```

The number of characters specified is too many for a punched card. Add 77 and 5, and the result is 82, but there are only 80 columns of data on a punched card. At runtime, the machine should indicate an error. Used with a WRITE statement for line printer output, the statement would be perfectly valid, since more than 82 printing positions will normally be available.

Here is another example of a FORMAT statement controlling several variables. We have to read in, from punched cards – using device number 5 – values for the four variables K, I, L and M. K and I can have at most three digits each, whereas L and M might be four-digit numbers. The four numbers are held on a single card in the following way:

K occupies columns 34 to 37, inclusive.

ɪ occupies columns 40 to 43, inclusive.
ʟ occupies columns 45 to 49, inclusive.
ᴍ is in columns 60 to 64.

Write an appropriate READ-FORMAT sequence, and compare it with the answer given below.

Here is my solution:

```
   READ (5, 2) K, I, L, M
 2 FORMAT (33X, I4, 2X, I4, 1X, I5, 10X, I5)
```

Note the use of ɪ4 to allow for the possibility of a negative three-digit number, and of ɪ5 to allow for a negative four-digit number. Often, one can omit the 'x' field specifications and use larger field specifications for the numeric items, knowing that they will be placed at the right-hand end of the field. The following is an alternative FORMAT statement, using this principle:

```
 2 FORMAT (33X, I4, I6, I6, I15)
```

or, more economically,

```
 2 FORMAT (33X, I4, 2I6, I15)
```

## Rescanning

The set of field specifications contained within the parentheses of the FORMAT statement is scanned from left to right, and when the final right parenthesis is encountered it implies that no further reading or printing is required on that card or line. If there is no more information to be transferred, the process of input or output will stop. If there is still information waiting to be transferred, a new line or input record will be started and, in the simple cases we have considered so far, the FORMAT statement will be *rescanned*, starting again at the left-most field specification. Later, we shall see that it is not always as simple as this.

## Record skipping

Just as the 'x' and 'ᴛ' specifications enable input characters to be ignored, or output spaces to be generated, there is a facility that enables complete input records to be skipped and completely blank lines to be produced. This is made possible by having a special character in the FORMAT specification that means 'the record (card or line) ends here'. Suppose that, in our previous example, K and I were on one card, and that L and M were on the next. The arrangement is shown in Fig. 11.1.

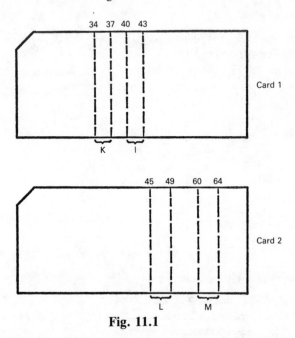

**Fig. 11.1**

We shall have to give instructions to read K and I from the first card and then ignore the rest of that card, taking the values of L and M from the second card. There are a number of ways in which this can be done, but the most straightforward is to use the following sequence:

```
      READ (5, 1) K, I
    1 FORMAT (33X, I4, 2X, I4)
C       REMEMBER — EACH READ STARTS A NEW RECORD
      READ (5, 2) L, M
    2 FORMAT (44X, I5, 10X, I5)
```

Here we have two reads to read two records, using the 'x' specification to skip over unwanted blanks within the record. Alternatively, we could use a single READ statement, but we should need to indicate in the FORMAT statement just where the end of the first record occurs. This is done by using the special separator mentioned above, which happens to be the slash ('/') character. The modified sequence is the following:

```
        READ (5, 10) K, I, L, M
   10 FORMAT (33X, I4, 2X, I4 / 44X, I5, 10X, I5)
```

Notice that, when a new record is started, the data line is scanned from column 1 again.

This method is often used for output also, but here a little care is needed. When a slash is used to indicate the end of a record (in this case, a line of output), the remainder of the information that is transferred has to go on a new line, or lines. It follows that the printer will need, for each printed line, control information in the form of the control character mentioned earlier, to ensure the correct positioning of the carriage. This control character will be the first transferred after the slash appears in the FORMAT statement.

In this next example, we output K, I, L and M to the printer in two lines, double spaced.

```
        WRITE (6,200) K, I, L, M
  200 FORMAT (11X, I4, 5X, I4 / '0', 9X, I5, 4X, I5)
```

The final tabulation should be:

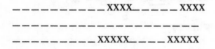

Again, the underlines represent spaces, and the 'x' characters represent printed digits (or spaces). Note how the single character '0' is included in the FORMAT statement as text that the printer will interpret as a control character to cause double spacing.

## Multiple skipping

If it is required to skip several records on input or output, more than one slash may be used. But their exact number depends on whether they will appear in the middle of a set of format specifications or at one end. If a group of *n* slashes appears at the beginning or end of a FORMAT list, then *n* records are skipped; if the *n* slashes appear in the middle of the list, then $n-1$ records are skipped. Thus, on input, the effect of the statement:

```
FORMAT (I6 / / I4, I5)
```

is to read a value from the first card, skip the next card, then read two values from the third card. The *two* slashes in the middle cause *one* card to be skipped. This is because the slash is an *end of record* indicator; the first slash indicates the end of information on the first card, the second slash indicates the end of information on the second card – even though none has been taken from it.

On output, the effect of the statement:

```
FORMAT ( 1X, I4, I5, I6, / / / )
```

is to print three values on the next line, then skip *three* lines. This is because the final right parenthesis of the FORMAT statement also acts as an end of record indicator (hence each read or write starts a new record), so we have an effective *four* record terminator, causing *three* to be skipped. Note that there is no need to separate the slashes by commas; indeed, in the example above, the comma after 'I6' is not needed, though it is not actually wrong to have it present. Note also the use of the '1x' specification, which sends a single space character as the first in the first record, to be used for carriage control ('print on the next line').

This statement:

```
FORMAT ( / / / 1X, I3, 10X, I7)
```

terminates *three* records – and so skips *three* lines – before causing the output of two values on the next line.

## Multiple and repeated field specifications

Here is an interesting sequence:

```
        READ (5, 100) (NUM(K), K=1, 20)
100 FORMAT (I10)
```

Does something seem a little wrong? You might well think so, for while the READ statement calls for the processing of 20 numbers, the FORMAT statement contains a field specification for only one number. But, in fact, all is well, and both statements are perfectly valid as the following explanation shows.

K will be assigned the value 1, and $NUM_1$ will be read in, using the field specification I10. Now the FORTRAN system has a problem; it has reached the extreme right-hand parenthesis of the FORMAT statement, but there are still 19 numbers left in the READ list ($NUM_2$ to $NUM_{20}$). There is really only one thing to do. The closing parenthesis is treated as an end-of-record indicator, and the set of field specifications is scanned backwards until an opening parenthesis is found. In this simple instance, there is only the one opening (i.e. left-hand) parenthesis, and when this is reached, the direction of the scan is reversed and input of values continues. Each scan of the FORMAT list results in the input of one value, until the READ list is exhausted. In our example, there will be 20 forward scans of the list, and so 20 numbers will be read *from 20 records*.

This rescanning principle can be extended to those cases in which there is more than one pair of parentheses in the FORMAT list. The following is an example of such an arrangement:

```
200  FORMAT (I10, I4 / (I8))
              *
```

When rescanning is required, the point from which the rescan starts is always the left parenthesis corresponding to the last-but-one right parenthesis. In our example, this is the one marked with an asterisk beneath it. If we now execute the statement:

```
READ (5, 200) I, J, (KOUNT(K), K=1, 15)
```

then I and J will be read from the first record, and the 15 elements of the array KOUNT will be taken one from each of the next 15 cards. This is because the rescanning process is 'looping' on that final (I8) specification. It will continue to do this until all the items of the READ list have been used up, and then the next statement will be obeyed.

Balanced parentheses are just as important in a FORMAT statement as they are anywhere else in a FORTRAN program. The number of closing parentheses must be exactly equal to the number of opening parentheses. When a field specification, or a set of field specifications, is repeated, we can save ourselves some writing effort by making use of *repetition* factors. Thus, instead of writing, for example,

```
300  FORMAT (I7, I7, I7, I8 / (I10))
```
we could write

```
300  FORMAT (3I7, I8 / (I10))
```

In the same way, we can abbreviate

```
555 FORMAT ('TABLE OF RESULTS' / / (I10, I5, I10, I5))
```

(which will be rescanned from the first 'I10', if necessary) to:

```
555 FORMAT ('TABLE OF RESULTS' / / 2(I10, I5))
```

This will be rescanned from the right-most left parenthesis, but the preceding *repetition factor* of 2 will be noted. The effect is the same as before.

## The colon in the FORMAT list

Sometimes, the information being transmitted runs out before all the FORMAT statement's field specifications have been used – this is most often the case when rescanning is being performed, since the number of items to be output is often not known. By using a colon, one can ensure that no further output is generated after the last data item has been transferred.

**Example**

```
      PRINT 450, (LINK(K), K=1, N)
  450 FORMAT (1X, I10 : / '0**********')
```

Here, the values of the array LINK are printed, one per line, with a line of asterisks beneath each one *except the last*; when the last value has been printed, the colon, in effect, prevents the string of asterisks being transmitted to the printer. Note the '0' at the head of the asterisk string – it is the control character that causes double spacing between number and asterisks. The following is typical output:

    123


**********
    −45678


**********
    2759

## Blanks or zeros?

In the last example given, although 10 print positions are allowed for each number printed, it will be noticed that those leading positions that are not used have been filled with spaces, rather than with zeros. In general, this gives the output much better readability and so it is what you will get unless you specify that you want something different. Nevertheless, you do have the choice in FORTRAN 77, for the output of integers. You can specify the minimum number of characters to be printed by following the number that represents the field width by a period and another number. So I10.6 would mean 'print as an integer in a field 10 characters wide, but at least 6 characters must be shown'. The three numbers in the last example would then be printed as:

_ _ _ _ 000123, _ _ _ _ −45678, and _ _ _ _ 002759.

When numbers are being read on input, it is, of course, quite normal that leading spaces (i.e. those preceding the first digit of the number) should be ignored. If an input field is completely blank, it is taken to contain zero. Usually, blank characters between digits, or at the right-hand end of the field, are ignored. It follows that the statements:

```
    READ (1, 250) I, J, K
250 FORMAT (I4, I5, I3)
```

given the following data, in which the underline again means 'space':

_ _ _ _ 12_3456_

would read the values as I = 0, J = 1234 and K = 56.

Within a particular FORMAT statement, this convention can be overridden, and one can specify that blanks be interpreted as zeros. This is done by using the format specification BZ (blanks are zero). Subsequent input data is then interpreted as though blanks in the number fields were zeros. If it is not to apply to all the numeric fields controlled by the FORMAT statement, it can be cancelled by the specification BN (blanks are null), which restores the normal convention. It is, in any case, automatically cancelled at the end of the FORMAT statement – or, rather, the input statement that makes use of the FORMAT statement.

If the FORMAT statement of our previous example is rewritten as:

```
250 FORMAT (I4, BZ, I5, BN, I3)
```

the values input will be I = 0, J = 12034 (the blank has become zero) and K = 56 (the BN cancelled the BZ, and so we have reverted to the conventional interpretation).

In general, if zeros are to be read, it is probably best to stick with the convention as far as *leading* spaces are concerned, but to ensure that any characters within the number that are meant to be read as zeros should be input as zeros.


## The F specification

When you want to print real numbers in their everyday representation, such as −27.346, this is the field specification to use. Naturally, it is also used to specify the format of real numbers on input.

The general form of the specification is:

F*w.d*

where w is the *total width* of the field containing the number, and *d* is the number of digits to be printed *after the decimal point*.

The phrase 'total width' is important. It includes all the digits of the number, both before and after the decimal point, and also an allowance of two character positions for the decimal point (which is *always* printed) and a possible negative sign (if the value is positive, no plus sign is printed, normally; this means that with a specification of, for example, F7.3, the range of printable values is from −99.999 up to 999.999 – the negative range is restricted because of the need to print the sign).

A little calculation should persuade you that w must always be at least 2 greater than *d*. There is a certain amount of freedom allowed to the designer of a FORTRAN compiler, in that he may choose whether or not the '0' preceding the decimal point is printed when a value is less than 1. If he has decided, for your system that this shall be the case, the minimum difference between w and *d* becomes 3. Obviously, if this is so, there can be no meaningful output if the total field width is less than three characters. If a field width is more than is needed to accommodate the value to be printed, the value will be printed right-adjusted in the field, which will be left-filled with spaces.

Consider this typical F specification: F9.3; it means that the required field width is nine print positions, and that there will be three digits printed after the decimal point. If the fraction part of the value is too large to be accommodated in the space allowed, the value will be *rounded* to fit. If the whole-number part is too big for the space allowed, an *overflow* condition exists: this will usually be indicated by the whole field being filled with asterisks, though some systems will automatically change to the 'G' format specification, which tries to give as much information as possible, within the limits of the field width.

Here are several values as they would be output using the F9.3 specification:

| Value | Prints as | |
|---|---|---|
| 0.0123456 | _ _ _ _0.012 | |
| 0.1234567 | _ _ _ _0.123 | |
| 1.2345678 | _ _ _ _1.235 | |
| 12.345678 | _ _ _12.346 | |
| 12345.678 | 12345.678 | |
| −234.5678 | _−234.568 | |
| −6.3 | _ _ _−6.300 | |
| −3456.789 | −3456.789 | |
| −12345.678 | ********* | (indicates overflow) |
| or, possibly, | −12345.68 | |
| 1234567.8 | ********* | |
| or, perhaps, | 1234567.8 | (if 'G' format is used) |

Of course, integer values output with the I specification can also be too large to fit in the given field width. In such a case, the field is normally filled with asterisks to indicate the overflow. For input of real numbers, the field width and number of decimal places may be indicated exactly as explained above, but there is an important difference: the field width is always given the meaning described previously, but the number of decimal places is used *only if no decimal point is given in the data field*. This allows numbers to be input without their decimal point, and thus more data can be packed into the input line. Or, in the UK, one might input values in pence, but read them as though there were two places of decimals and hence store the values as pounds and fractions of a pound. In the USA, one might similarly read cent values to be stored as dollar amounts. The exact position of the decimal point is defined by the *d* parameter of the field specification.

Thus, given this set of data:

12345678901234567890

and this FORMAT statement:

```
FORMAT (F8.4, F6.2, F6.3)
```

the three values read from the data record will be +1234.5678, +9012.34 and +567.890.

Many people, however, like their data to be more readable than this, so that it can be checked by eye. They will be relieved to know that the decimal point may be punched and, whatever the value of the *d* parameter, the actual number of decimal places typed or punched will override that value. So, given this data record:

123.456.789.0

and this FORMAT statement:

```
FORMAT (F7.0, F3.1, F3.2)
```

the values read will be +123.456, +0.78 and +9.0. The number of decimal places, in each case, is that actually appearing in the field.

Here is a final example. It is required to input the value of a variable, A(I), which is expected to be less than 1000. The decimal point will be punched, and the number field begins at column 12 on the card. The value will never be negative, but there may be up to six places of decimals. Since the value will always be positive or zero, there is no need to allow room for the sign. We shall need room for, at most, three digits before the decimal point and six after it – a total of 10 characters. F10.6 should be a satisfactory field specification, then. But F10.0 would have been equally good, since the decimal point will always be physically present in the data. Indeed, any of F10.0, F10.1, F10.2, . . . would serve. My preference is for F10.0, and so is that of many other FORTRAN programmers. We shall also need to skip over the first 11 columns, since the data field starts in column 12.

The following should be all right:

```
      READ (5, 45) A(I)
45 FORMAT (11X, F10.0)
```

## The E specification

'E' stands for 'exponent', and a number output using this field specification will be in exponent (i.e. scientific or floating-point) form. As far as input is concerned, the E specification may be taken as equivalent to the F specification having the same field width. Numbers output in this way will generally look like this:

$\pm 0$ .xxxxxxxxE$\pm$yy

Sometimes they will look like this (when 'yy' is a number exceeding 99):

$\pm 0$.xxxxxxxx$\pm$yyy

These are floating-point numbers, in which each 'x' represents a digit in the *mantissa* (or fraction part) of the number, and each 'y' represents a digit in the integer *exponent*. The number has a true value given by x * 10 ** y (using FORTRAN notation), where x is the mantissa value and y is the exponent value. By representing numbers in this way, a very wide range of values can be accommodated, at the expense of a little speed and some slight but controllable loss of accuracy. If the mantissa is negative, it will be preceded by a minus sign; if not, the plus sign will be suppressed and replaced by a space. The exponent is always signed, even when positive.

The general form of this specification is

E*w.d*

where *w* is the total field width and *d* is the number of digits wanted in the mantissa, after the decimal point.

There are seven positions in any floating-point number that must be filled before we start thinking about the mantissa. These are: the sign of the mantissa, the digit preceding the decimal point, the decimal point itself, and the four characters that constitute the exponent part of the number. It follows that the minimum field width must be eight characters, for a number such as $-0.1$E$+02$, representing the value 10. Many beginning (and other!) FOR-TRAN programmers overlook this, and get some strange output as a result.

A typical number output in this form would be 0.154376E−01, which represents the value 0.0154376, and might have been printed using the field specification E13.6 (13 character positions in total, six significant figures). Numbers input in this form can be read using an E field specification.

If the absolute value of the exponent is likely to exceed 999, an alternative form of the E specification must be used:

E*w*.*d*E*e*

in which *e* represents the number of digits to be printed in the exponent part of the number.

Here are the same values as were used for the F specification examples, but using E specifications.

| Value | Field specification | Prints as |
|-------|---------------------|-----------|
| 0.0123456 | E13.6 | _0.123456E−01 |
| 0.1234567 | E11.7 | *********** |
| 1.2345678 | E14.6E3 | _ _0.123457+001 |
| 12.345678 | E14.6E4 | _0.123457+0002 |
| 12345.678 | E14.7 | _0.1234568E+05 |
| −234.5678 | E14.7 | −0.2345678E+03 |
| −6.3 | E9.1 | _ −0.6E+01 |
| −3456.789 | E13.7 | ************* |
| −12345.678 | E12.4 | _ −0.1235E+05 |
| 1234567.8 | E15.8 | _0.12345678E+07 |

## The A specification

We have already met CHARACTER variables and constants, and seen that, if TX is a character constant of sufficient size, a statement such as

```
TX = 'ERROR'
```

is quite acceptable. Very often, however, we should like to read text strings in from the input device and store the data in character variables. Equally, there is a frequent need to print as text the content of one or more character variables. This may be achieved by using 'A' field specifications.

The general form of the specification is:

A*w*

where *w* is the field width of the item on the input or output medium. Let us first consider input of character data. We shall assume the declarations

```
CHARACTER T1, T2 * 2, T3 * 3, T4 * 4
```

and the input record consists of the character string:

ABCDE12345

If we now execute the statement

```
      READ (5, 100) T1, T2, T3, T4
100   FORMAT (A1, A2, A3, A4)
```

we shall get the result T1 ='A', T2 ='BC', T3 ='DE1' and T4 ='2345'. Remember: there is a world of difference between the character constant '2345' and the integer value 2345.

In this example the data fields were of exactly the same size as the character variables to which the data items were moved. If the sizes differ, there are rules for determining what happens. Suppose the field specification is A*w* and the size of the receiving variable is *n* characters.

When *w* is greater than *n*, the problem is akin to squeezing a quart into a pint pot. It is the right-most *n* characters that are transferred. When *w* is smaller than *n*, we have room to spare. The character string is moved into the left-hand end of the variable, and the rest of the variable is filled up with spaces.

A more general field specification may be used – simply the single letter 'A' with no field width given. In this case, the number of characters transferred is exactly equal to the number that the variable can hold. Using the same input record as before, the statements

```
      READ (5, 200) T1, T2, T3, T4
200   FORMAT (A3, 2A, A2)
```

will result in: T1 = 'C', T2 = 'DE', T3 = '123' and T4 = '45__', in which – as usual – the underline character _ has been used to represent the space character.

On *output*, similar considerations apply. When *w* exceeds *n*, there is more space available than is needed. The *n* characters are output at the right-hand end of the field, preceded by the appropriate number of spaces.

When *w* is less than *n*, the data item is too large to be fitted into the field. If we are outputting a number, the field would be filled with asterisks to indicate the overflow (obviously a necessity, since lost digits can cause serious problems – imagine receiving a cheque for £000 when you were expecting one for £1000! If £*** had been printed, someone might have noticed it earlier). In the output of text, however, overflow may not be quite so important; indeed, one may quite intentionally decide to select part of the text for printing. In this case it is the left-most *w* characters from the variable that are used to fill the available space on the output medium.

The simple 'A' specification can also be used for output. When this is done, the *n* characters are output from the variable to the next *n* positions on the output medium.

**Example**

Given the following character variables, with the contents shown:

| Variable | Size | Value |
|----------|------|-------|
| P | 3 | 'ABC' |
| Q | 4 | '1234' |
| R | 5 | 'PQRST' |

the statement

```
WRITE (6, '(1X, A4, 1X, A3, 1X, A)') P, Q, R
```

(note how the format list has, in this example, been 'embedded' in the control information list of the WRITE statement – a useful feature if the format is only to be used once, saving a FORMAT statement and the reference to it) produces, as output,

_ABC_123_PQRST

## The L specification

The input and output of LOGICAL values is achieved by using the 'L' field specification. The general form of the specification is

L*w*

in which, again, *w* is the field width. On input, leading spaces in the field are ignored. If the first non-blank character is 'T', or '.' followed by 'T', the value .TRUE. is assigned to the variable. If it is 'F', or '.' followed by 'F', the value .FALSE. is assigned. Remaining characters in the field are ignored

**Example**

Given a field specification of L10, for the data items given, the values shown will be assigned:

| Data field | Value read |
|------------|------------|
| .FALSE.___ | .FALSE. |
| ___.FALSE. | .FALSE. |
| __TRUE____ | .TRUE. |
| _FREDDIE__ | .FALSE. |
| ____T_____ | .TRUE. |

On output, the letter 'T' (for .TRUE.) or 'F' (for .FALSE.) is placed in the right-most position of the receiving field.

**Example**

```
      READ *, X
      NEGX = X .LT. 0.0
C     IT IS ASSUMED THAT NEGX HAS BEEN DECLARED
C     LOGICAL
      WRITE ( *, 100) X, NEGX
100   FORMAT ('0', F10.4, L6)
```

If the value read for x is $-35.76548$, the output will be

```
_____
__−35.7655_____T
```

If the value of x had been 274.25, the output would have been

```
_____
__274.2500_____F
```

## The D specification

This is the means by which numbers declared as being DOUBLE PRECISION may be output or input. For all practical purposes, its action is the same as that of the E specification in its E*w.d* form, except that one writes D*w.d* (*w* being the field width and *d* the number of digits in the mantissa). On output, the exponent will be preceded by a 'D' instead of an 'E'.

## Sign language

We have so far assumed that when a value to be output is positive, the sign is suppressed and a space printed in its place. This is a normal convention, but the designers of FORTRAN 77 left it open to the compiler writers to do it either in that way *or* by printing the sign. Whichever way it is implemented, almost certainly there will be a user who wants it the other way round. For that reason, there is a format facility for control of the printing of the plus sign.

Like BZ and BN, this applies only to the output statement using the format statement in which the control characters appear. When that is completed, sign output reverts to the system convention.

SP is used to indicate that plus signs must be printed ss to indicate that they must be replaced by spaces. The single letter s restores the system convention. Thus, if plus signs are normally suppressed,

```
WRITE(*, '(1X, ''BALANCE IS '',SP,F10.2//)')TOTAL
```

will tell you (positively!) when your account is healthy.

## Exercises

1 Write a subroutine subprogram to convert polar coordinates R and THETA to the corresponding Cartesian coordinates X and Y, using the formulae

$$X = R \cos \text{THETA}, \quad Y = R \sin \text{THETA}.$$

Incorporate the subroutine in a program to tabulate the corresponding values of X and Y for a curve whose polar equation is

$$R = 2 \cos \text{THETA}$$

for values of THETA from 0° to 360° in steps of 10°.

The relationship between degrees and radians is that $1° = 0.0174533$ radians. Tabulate R, THETA, X and Y for each point, using F specifications for X and Y (4 decimal places), and E specification for R (6 significant figures). THETA should be printed as an integer.

2 Write a program that reads two logical values input as 'TRUE' or 'FALSE' and prints, as 'T' or 'F' their non-equivalence, defined as TRUE if the two values are different, FALSE otherwise.

3 Write a function subprogram that has a single integer argument in the range 1 to 7 and returns a character string with the name of the corresponding day of the week (1 = SUNDAY). Use it in a program that reads in a day number followed by the letter 'T' or 'F' and prints a message such as

    IT IS FRIDAY, AND THE SUN IS SHINING

for the data

    6T

or

    IT IS WEDNESDAY, AND THE SUN IS NOT SHINING

for the data

    4F

4 The results from a certain program are to be printed. At their head, centred on the line so far as possible, the following is to be printed:

    LIST OF SUSPECTED PERSONS

Then five lines are to be skipped and on the next line, on the extreme right-hand end:

    PAGE:__xxx

(where xxx represents the value of the variable PAGNO, an integer whose value is in the range 1 to 999).

Skip five more lines and print in the centre of the line:

    XXXXXXXXXXXXXXXXXXXXX REGION

where the xs are the name of a region held in the character variable AREA.

Write the appropriate FORTRAN 77 statements for an 80-character line

5 True or false?

 (a) All the print positions of a 132-column line printer are available for printing.

 (b) Every READ and WRITE statement must have its own FORMAT statement.

 (c) All FORMAT statements must be labelled (with a statement number).

 (d) A FORMAT statement must always be the next statement in a program following the WRITE statement.

 (e) A READ statement may have an empty list.

 (f) It is not permitted to mix real and integer variables in the same READ or WRITE list.

 (g) The output field specification F9.2 implies that the number being output has seven digits, of which two come after the decimal point.

# 12

# More input and output – files and things

We have seen that the basic data unit for input and output is the *record*, which consists of a number of data items held in the *fields* of the record. A collection of such records, all of the same type, is called a *file*.

There may be many records in a file, and different files will contain different types of record. For example, a doctor will maintain a file of patients' records, each of which contains, among other things, the name, date of birth and address of one patient; or a storekeeper in the spare parts department of a garage has access to a parts file containing, for each spare part, its reference number, description and price; again, a library catalogue is a file, each record referring to a single book and containing details of the title, author, accession number, classification code, etc.

Files are usually ordered in one way or another, so as to make it easier for the user to fined information. The doctor's file may be ordered alphabetically on the patients' surnames; the parts file is probably in ascending order of part number; and the library catalogue is likely to be duplicated as two files, one arranged in alphabetical order of author's name, the other in ascending order by classification code.

## File processing

There are basically two ways in which we can get at (*access* is the accepted term) a particular record within a file. The first approach is to start at the beginning of the file and examine each record in turn until we find the one we are seeking. (We shall recognise it because it will have one particular data item, or a group of them, called the record *key*, which is unique to that record. For example, in the library file, author plus title will usually form a unique key that identifies a book; in the garage, the part number will be sufficient to identify a particular spare part record; the doctor can probably use the patient's full name plus birth date as the key for his record system.)

This method of finding records is called *sequential* access, because each is examined in sequence, until the required record is located. The sequential method is fine for short files, or for those in which almost every record has to be dealt with. When the file is much larger and relatively few records are to be processed in each scan, an alternative access method is preferable. It is called *direct* access, because if we know the record key – as, of course, we should – we can go directly to that part of the file – even, often, the exact record of the file – in which we are interested, without having to examine the key fields of all the records that precede it in the file. This can lead to a considerable saving in processing time for large files.

## File media

FORTRAN 77 gives its users the option of organising and accessing files either sequentially or directly. For direct access, however, it is necessary to know the *position* of the record within the file. Real-life files tend to be large, needing a great deal of storage capacity. The internal, or *immediate-access*, memory of a computer tends to be relatively small and is often reserved for the storage of programs and their intermediate results. Thus, files are usually held in the computer's *backing* or *auxiliary* storage area, which is of high capacity but is (relatively) slow to access. The term 'slow' here means anything from, say, 0.01 to 200 seconds, depending on the storage medium used, as compared to, perhaps, 0.0000005 seconds for the main memory. Typically, such auxiliary storage would involve a magnetic medium; the simplest would use *magnetic tape*, and the more sophisticated some form of *magnetic disc* system. The physical details are not important here; suffice to say that files held on magnetic tape are, by the very nature of the medium, of a sequential nature, and the only convenient way to process them is by using a sequential access method. Files held on magnetic disc, on the other hand, may usually be processed either sequentially or directly. It follows that, for fast access to file data, the magnetic disc is preferred. This has to be balanced against the fact that magnetic tape is a somewhat less expensive medium in use.

## Files and FORTRAN

For security reasons, computer files need *labels*. Sticky labels are, naturally, used for external identification, but each file will generally have a *label record* – the first record of the file – which contains, among other things, the name of the file (which should be unique), so that any attempt to use the file can be checked to ensure that the correct file has, in fact, been loaded. Other items in the label record include the date of creation of the file, the date beyond which it is no longer required, etc. A similar 'trailer' record is usually to be found at the end of the file if it is sequentially organised, together with a special *end of file* record.

When a program wishes to use a file, the first operation to be performed is that of *opening* the file. This can often be done before the program is started – if this is so for your installation, the details will be found in the appropriate manual – but FORTRAN 77 has an OPEN command that allows this to be done by program. Opening involves establishing a connection between the named file and the physical unit on which it is mounted, so that subsequent references to that device number are treated as references to the file, checking that the file mounted is really the one specified by the programmer, indicating the type of access (sequential or direct) required, the direction of data transfer (input or output), and so on.

When a program has finished using a file, it may be 'closed', using the CLOSE command, which makes it inaccessible unless another OPEN command is executed.

## Unformatted input and output

A statement such as

```
WRITE (9) A, B, C
```

causes the values of A, B and C to be written to the file on device number 9 in a machine-readable format. This method is frequently used when the output is not for human consumption, but will eventually be re-input for further processing. In general, these *unformatted records* will occupy less space than the formatted ones with which we have exclusively dealt so far. They are re-input by a precisely similar READ statement:

```
READ (9) A, B, C
```

will bring the original values back into the named variables. The names could, of course, have been changed, but their *types* (REAL, CHARACTER, etc.) should be the same.

Note that no FORMAT reference should be given, but that the END and ERR control list items may be used.

## The END FILE **statement**

The simple statement

```
END FILE n
```

where *n* is a device number or an integer variable whose value is a valid device number, will cause an end of file record to be written on that device if it is a sequential output file.

An alternative form of the statement is this:

```
END FILE (UNIT = n, ERR = label, IOSTAT = var)
```

in which *label* is a statement number, *var* is an integer variable name, and *n* is, as before, a device number.

These three items may appear in any order, and only the UNIT specifier is obligatory. However, if – as is permissible – the words 'UNIT =' are omitted, the device number must appear first within the parentheses. If the ERR specifier is present, then control will be transferred to the given statement number if an error occurs when an attempt is made to write the end of file record. If the IOSTAT specifier is present, and no error condition arises, the variable named will be set to a value of zero. In the event of an error when attempting to write the end of file record, the variable will be set to a positive value that will give an indication of the type of the error. This will vary from one installation to another: consult your system reference manual. The following are typical END FILE commands:

```
END FILE 7
END FILE (7)
END FILE (7, ERR = 123)
END FILE (7, ERR = 4567, IOSTAT = KLUDGE)
END FILE (UNIT = 7, IOSTAT = IWRONG, ERR = 9999)
END FILE (IOSTAT = MESS, UNIT = 6, ERR = 1212)
```

There is not much point in using IOSTAT without ERR, since the program will simply abort in the event of an error – you will have lost control and whatever value the IOSTAT variable might have received will be lost also. 'ERR', of course, means 'error', 'IOSTAT' means 'input/output status'.

## The OPEN statement

The general form of this statement is:

OPEN (list of specifiers)

The specifier list is similar to that used with the END FILE statement, except that there are more of them. There must be a device number, indicated by UNIT = $n$, where $n$ is a valid device number, as before. Again, the words 'UNIT =' can be omitted, but if this is done $n$ must be the first item inside the parentheses.

It is worth noting that there are basically three ways in which one can use a file: it may already exist and one is using the data it contains or updating that information; one may be creating a new file, so the file does not – at the time of opening – exist; one may intend to use a file for 'scratch-pad' purposes, writing some records to it, perhaps reading them back again, but eventually discarding it (this is called a 'scratch' file). One of the OPEN specifiers is intended to enable us to give this information about the file. The word STATUS = may be followed by one of four character strings (the quotes are required!).

| | |
|---|---|
| 'OLD' | means that the file already exists. |
| 'NEW' | means that the file does not yet exist and is to be created. |
| 'SCRATCH' | means that the file may be discarded when the program ends. |
| 'UNKNOWN' | means that the system must search its file directory |

and discover the status of this file for itself. If a file of the given name already exists, the status will be 'OLD', but if not, one will be created with status 'NEW'

If a file has status 'OLD', it *must* exist. If not, an error occurs. Obviously, a name for the file must be given. If a file has status 'NEW', no file of that name must exist: if it does, an error occurs. A file specified as SCRATCH must not be given a name.

Naming is achieved by the specifier FILE = followed by the name of the file (which must conform to the file-naming conventions of your computer system). The name must be enclosed in quotes.

Here are some simple OPEN statements:

```
OPEN (8, FILE = 'SALES')
```

This opens a file called 'SALES' on unit 8. By default, its status is 'UNKNOWN' and must be determined by the system.

```
OPEN (FILE = 'SALES', UNIT = 8)
```

Exactly the same, but the full 'UNIT =' specifier is needed, since it is not the first in the list.

```
OPEN (9, STATUS = 'SCRATCH')
OPEN (7, FILE = 'LASTWEEK',
*      STATUS = 'OLD', ERR = 99)
```

The ERR specifier acts in the same way as in END FILE.

```
OPEN (12, FILE = 'CUSTO1', STATUS = 'NEW',
*          ERR = 444, IOSTAT = NASTY)
```

So does IOSTAT. Do not be afraid to use continuations to maintain readability in long statements like this.

In all the above examples, because nothing to the contrary was stated, it will be assumed that the files are sequential and that formatted input and output are to be used. We can alter that by using other specifiers, as follows.

ACCESS =     'SEQUENTIAL'   (for sequential access)
       or 'DIRECT'       (for direct access)

It is important to realise that you can only use the access modes that your computer system permits; if direct access file handling is not implemented on your system, specifying it in a FORTRAN 77 program will not make it happen.

The default acess mode is, as mentioned earlier, 'SEQUENTIAL'.

FORM =     'FORMATTED'      (if the records are formatted)
     or   'UNFORMATTED'    (if the records are unformatted)

Here the default value depends on the access mode. Unless there is a FORM specifier, it is assumed that 'SEQUENTIAL' files are 'FORMATTED', 'DIRECT' files are 'UNFORMATTED'.

For direct access files, the facility to declare the length of a record exists, using the specifier RECL = followed by the length of the record in characters:

```
OPEN (7, FILE = 'MESSAGES', ACCESS = 'DIRECT',
*      ERR = 999, IOSTAT = KERR,
*      FORM = 'FORMATTED', RECL = 80,
*      STATUS = 'OLD')
```

Finally, it is possible to determine the way in which blank characters will be handled in the numeric fields of formatted records. The specifier

BLANK = 'ZERO'   will cause all blanks to be read as zeros.
BLANK = 'NULL'   will result in blanks being ignored, except that a completely blank field will be read as a zero.

## The CLOSE statement

This is a statement used to disconnect a file from the device to which it is connected (usually by an OPEN statement). It has the form:

CLOSE (list)

in which *list* is a list of specifiers similar to those of the OPEN and END FILE statements. CLOSE is used when a file is no longer needed for access during the program. The specifiers used in the list are UNIT =, ERR = and IOSTAT =; these three have exactly the same meanings as in the OPEN and END FILE statements, and also STATUS= which has two possible values:

STATUS =     'KEEP'    means the file is to be retained after the program terminates. This is the default value; it may not be used for scratch files.
       or   'DELETE'  means that the file is to be deleted.

**Examples**

CLOSE (10)    Close the file on unit 10, and keep it if it was not a
             scratch file.

```
CLOSE (UNIT = 11, ERR = 999, STATUS = 'DELETE')
```

## Reading from and writing to files

For *sequential* input and output, given that the file has been opened
appropriately, the READ and WRITE statements we have already
considered are quite adequate, as long as the appropriate device is
used. We have, in effect, been reading from a sequential file (the
terminal's string of characters or that from the card reader) and
writing to one (the VDU screen or the line printer), so there is
nothing new to say. Two statements for positioning the file are
worth a mention, however.

The command

BACKSPACE *n*

causes the file on device *n* to be positioned so that the next record
read is that which has just been read: it is spaced backward one
complete record position. The alternative is

BACKSPACE (*list*)

in which *list* is a list of specifiers selected from UNIT =, ERR = and
IOSTAT =, all with the same meanings as before and used in the same
way.

The command

REWIND *n*

or

REWIND (*list*)

in which *n* and *list* have the same meanings as before, causes the file
to be positioned such that the next record read is the first of the file
(i.e. it is positioned as it would be immediately after the execution
of the OPEN command).

BACKSPACE and REWIND cannot be applied to the standard input
and output devices.

For *direct* access to files, it is necessary to realise that each record has a unique position in the file, and that the records are numbered from 1 upward in steps of 1. Thus, a file of five records would contain record 1, record 2, record 3, record 4, and record 5, in that order. We can indicate precisely which record of a file is to be read by including in the READ statement a specifier that gives the number of the record wanted, thus:

```
READ (8, REC = 43, ERR = 777) (A(I), I=1, 10)
```

This statement reads from the forty-third record of the file on device number 8, 10 real values into the first 10 elements of the array A. The read is unformatted, but need not have been if the file had been opened as 'FORMATTED'.

In a similar way, one may write data into any specified record position:

```
WRITE(8, REC = 98, ERR = 778)
*       P, Q, R, S, (T(I), I = 5, 10)
```

For a given file, of course, the form of the data in the record is fixed – in this case, 10 REAL values. Here we have written 10 values into record position 98.

## Exercises

1  A formatted sequential file contains records each consisting of a six-character (possibly negative) integer, followed by a string of 122 alphanumeric characters. Write a program that will read this file (called 'MASTER') and split it between two other sequential files, 'TEMP1' and 'TEMP2', in such a way that those records that start with a positive number are written to 'TEMP1' and those starting with a negative number go to 'TEMP2'.

2  After executing the program of question 1, above, the file 'TEMP1' will consist only of those records having a positive number in the first field. This is now to be treated as the key field, the file being read and rewritten to a direct access file called 'D1', each record being stored in the record position given by its numeric field. The file 'D1' may not, however, contain records whose key exceeds 9999. Any such records are to be listed on the line printer, and not copied to 'D1'. The line printer is device number 6 and prints 132 characters per line.

# 13

# Left-overs

This chapter contains information about, with one exception, a number of the features of FORTRAN that are somewhat less important but that, nevertheless, one will encounter sufficiently often for them not to be completely omitted. The exception – which has been left until now because it did not seem to fit naturally anywhere else – is the means by which initial values can be given to variables at the time the program is loaded (i.e. brought into memory, ready to be executed).

## The DATA statement

We have seen how the PARAMETER statement may be used to establish constant named values that may not then be changed during the running of the program. The DATA initialisation statement is very similar in effect, except that the assigned values can be changed at runtime.

It is often useful to have values assigned to some of the program's variables at the beginning of execution of a program unit. This can save the writing of a long string of assignment statements. For instance, if it is required to assign the values 1.3, 2.7, 10 and 16 to the variables A, B, I and J, respectively, the simple approach is to write four assignments:

```
A = 1.3
B = 2.7
I = 10
J = 16
. . .
```

This can be very tedious to write and keypunch when the list is a long one, and will need time to execute at runtime. The alternative is to use a *data initialisation* statement; the following example will achieve the desired assignments at the time the program unit is loaded.

```
DATA A/1.3/, B/2.7/, I/10/, J/16/
```

The general form of the statement is:

DATA *varlist* / *vallist* /, *varlist* / *vallist* / , . . . etc.

in which each *varlist* is a different list of variable names, and each *vallist* is a list of their values. The values are assigned to the variables strictly in the order of their appearance. The variables may be subscripted. The last list of values must be terminated by a slash, but no terminal comma is needed. In the example, each list contains only one variable or value, but this need not be the case. We could rewrite it in a number of ways. Here are two possibilities:

```
DATA A, B, I, J / 1.3, 2.7, 10, 16 /
DATA A, B / 1.3, 2.7 / , I, J / 10, 16 /
```

The most compact method is probably that in which there is a single list of variables followed by the corresponding list of values.

When several variables are to be given the same value, a short-hand form of the value list may be used:

```
DATA A, B, C, D, E, F, G / 3 * 0.0, 4 * 10.0 /
```

This causes the first *three* variables A, B and C to be given the value 0.0, and the remaining *four* will receive the value 10.0.

When array elements are being initialised, the implied DO construction may be used. The following has the effect of initialising all the 35 elements of the LOGICAL array PAID to the value .FALSE.

```
DATA (PAID(I), I = 1, 35) / 35 * .FALSE. /
```

Notice that 35 elements are named, in effect, and so 35 values must be specified. To give a different set of initial values to the elements of, say, the array XVALS, one could write:

```
DATA (XVALS(J), J = 1, 5) /1.0,2.0,3.0,4.0,5.0 /
```

One of the problems with the DATA statement is that it may not be used to initialise values held in blank common. It may, however, be used to give initial values to variables held in *named* common storage, but this must be done in a separate subprogram, called the *block data* subprogram. There may not be more than one block data subprogram per FORTRAN job. It always has the heading statement:

```
BLOCK DATA
```

followed by the COMMON statements and any necessary specification (INTEGER, REAL, DOUBLE PRECISION, COMPLEX, LOGICAL, CHARACTER, DIMENSION, etc.) statements. Finally, the necessary DATA statements are given, and the subprogram finishes with an END statement. A block data subprogram *never* contains executable statements – those which specify actions to be taken at runtime; its purpose is solely to initialise the values of variables in common storage at load time.

A typical BLOCK DATA subprogram might look like the following:

```
BLOCK DATA
COMMON /QXABF/ A(2), IBOUT, JBOUT, B(2), IBUF
LOGICAL A, B
DATA A(1), A(2), B(1), B(2), IBUF, IBOUT, JBOUT/
*       .TRUE., .TRUE., .FALSE., .FALSE., 0, 7, 8/
END
```

This gives the indicated initial values to the variables held in the named common block, QXABF. The elements of the logical arrays A and B are initialised to .TRUE. and .FALSE., respectively, and the three integer variables IBUF, IBOUT and JBOUT receive the values 0, 7 and 8, respectively. Character variables could be similarly initialised, though, you will recall, they must be in a separate named common block. It is not necessary to initialise *all* the variables in a block.

## The IMPLICIT statement

We have seen that there are certain conventions in the naming of FORTRAN real and integer variables which, if they are used, mean that the explicit declaration of the type of those variables is not necessary. Integers have names beginning with I, J, K, L, M or N, and reals have names whose first letter is one of those remaining. This often results in names such as JBUFF, KVALUE, XMEAN and RNUM which lose a certain amount of their readability because of the need to use a first letter that is not naturally a part of the word. This can be overcome by using the REAL and INTEGER declarations to override the convention; in the example given, two statements might be used:

```
REAL MEAN, NUM
INTEGER BUFF, VALUE
```

Occasionally, however, it is found that there are a large number of variables of a particular type in a program unit, that it is inconvenient to name all in accordance with the convention and that it is an onerous task to have to declare the name of each one in a type statement. Thus, for example, one may be writing a program in which there is no real arithmetic – all the variables are integers. We can, of course, use the convention and have a proliferation of unreadable names that conform to the convention. Alternatively, we can use the names we want, and which are meaningful, but if we do so we shall have to declare them in an INTEGER declaration. There is now a third possibility; the statement

```
IMPLICIT INTEGER (A - Z)
```

specifies that all variables beginning with the letters A, B, C, . . . Z are to be treated as of integer type; in other words, all the program unit's variables, whatever they are called.

The normal FORTRAN naming convention is as though the declarations

```
IMPLICIT INTEGER (I - N)
IMPLICIT REAL (A - H, O - Z)
```

had been included in the program unit. Note that two or more ranges of letters can appear in such a statement.

The convention for naming variables only applies to those of REAL and INTEGER types; the others – DOUBLE PRECISION, COMPLEX, LOGICAL, CHARACTER – all need explicit declaration, and such declarations obviously override the convention. We could decide that, in a particular program unit, all double-precision variables should have names beginning with 'D', all complex variables should start their names with 'C', logical variables with 'L', and character variables with 'S' (for 'string'). Nothing could now be simpler, though we must bear in mind that these letters are no longer available for naming reals or integers. We shall need four IMPLICIT statements:

```
  IMPLICIT DOUBLE PRECISION (D), COMPLEX (C),
*            LOGICAL (L), CHARACTER * 6 (S)
```

As you can see, several declarations of implicit type can be combined into a single IMPLICIT statement. You will note that a CHARACTER declaration has to imply the number of characters in the declared entities, so a length specifier has been included. If strings of a different length are to be handled, they will have to be declared separately. Note also that the naming conventions thus established (a) apply only within the program unit (main program, subroutine, function or block data subprogram) in which the IMPLICIT statement appears, and (b) will apply to any function names that are used – so a little extra care is needed.

## The ordering of statements

Although many types of statement have been dealt with in the course of this book, little advice has been given as to their ordering (except, of course, for the executable statements that implement the algorithm). There is, none the less, a fairly firm requirement as to the order in which the non-executable statements are written, within the general pattern of: first, the program unit's header statement (PROGRAM, SUBROUTINE, FUNCTION or BLOCK DATA); second, specifications and declarations; third, statement function declarations; and, finally, the executable instructions, finishing up with the END statement. DATA statements may not appear within the first two groups, and PARAMETER statements *must*, if used, be in the second group. Within that second group, IMPLICIT statements must precede any other variable declarations and specifications. FORMAT statements can appear anywhere between the heading and the END statement. The above may be clarified by Fig. 13.1, based on that given in the American National Standard.

The ENTRY statement is not dealt with in this book and is of little importance. The specification statements are, in summary: IMPLI-CIT, PARAMETER, DIMENSION, COMMON, EQUIVALENCE, EXTERNAL, INTRINSIC, SAVE, REAL, INTEGER, DOUBLE PRECISION, COMPLEX, LOGICAL, CHARACTER. Of these the last six are also termed *declarations*, or *type statements*.

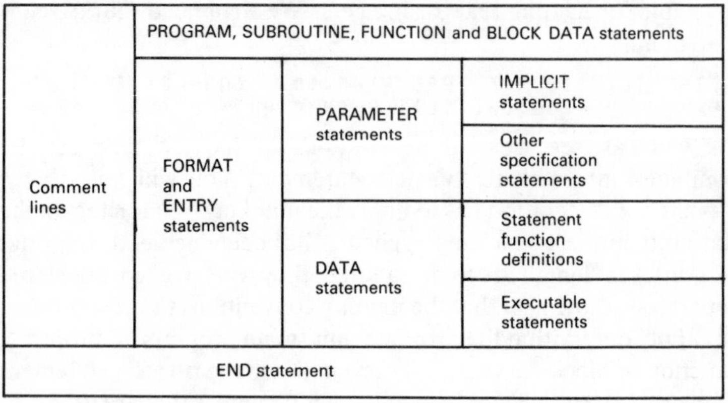

| Comment lines | PROGRAM, SUBROUTINE, FUNCTION and BLOCK DATA statements | | |
|---|---|---|---|
| | FORMAT and ENTRY statements | PARAMETER statements | IMPLICIT statements |
| | | | Other specification statements |
| | | DATA statements | Statement function definitions |
| | | | Executable statements |
| END statement | | | |

**Fig. 13.1**

The purpose of the SAVE statement is to ensure that the values of the local variables named in the list that follows it, as in

```
SAVE X, Y, Z
```

(X, Y and Z are referenced only within the subprogram) are preserved between one call of a subprogram and the next. If this is not done, there is no guarantee that the values will not have changed between calls. The reason for this is rather involved, but is to do with the way in which the system allocates its storage. One possible application might be to maintain a count of the number of times a subprogram is entered, like this:

```
SUBROUTINE S(A, B)
INTEGER COUNT
SAVE COUNT
DATA COUNT /0/
COUNT = COUNT + 1
...
END
```

The DATA statement ensures that COUNT is initialised to zero when the program is first loaded, but without the SAVE statement the value of COUNT becomes undefined after the return to the calling routine, and the next time S is called the attempt to change COUNT's value could cause an error condition. SAVE prevents this happening.

# The 'arithmetic' IF statement

This statement is a way of achieving a three-way branch with a single instruction. It has become somewhat unfashionable in recent years, among computer scientists, because its use can lead to badly structured programs, but it has always been a favourite of the engineer and scientist who writes his own programs. In case you meet, or need it, it has the general form

IF $(exp)$ $s_1$, $s_2$, $s_3$

in which *exp* is an arithmetic expression, and $s_1$, $s_2$ and $s_3$ are statement numbers. The expression is first evaluated; the result is a value that is in one of three ranges. If it is less than zero, a branch is made to the statement labelled with $s_1$; if it is greater than zero, the branch is to $s_3$; if the expression has a value exactly equal to zero, the branch is made to $s_2$. The three statement numbers may be all different, or any two may be the same, thus allowing for 'equal/not equal', 'greater than or equal' and 'less than or equal' tests.

A very simple example would be:

```
IF (Q) 10, 20, 30
```

meaning 'examine the value of Q and branch to label 10 if it is negative, 30 if it is positive, and 20 if it is zero'.

But we can use *any* arithmetic expression:

```
IF (B**2 - 4*A*C) 100, 150, 200
```

takes us to label 100 if the expression is negative (i.e. $B^2$ is less than $4AC$), to 150 if it has the value zero, and to 200 if it is positive. Remember that the statement immediately after the arithmetic IF will itself need a statement number: without one, it will be unreachable!

# Answers to the exercises

**Chapter 2**

1

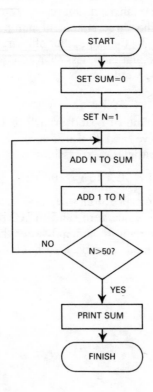

2

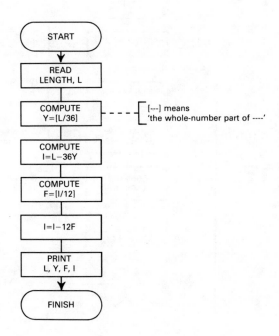

3

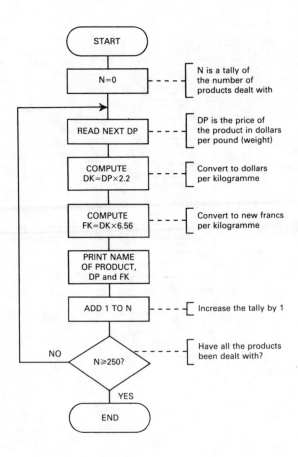

4

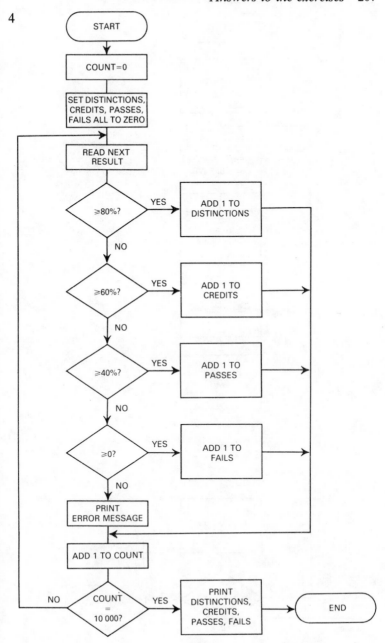

5

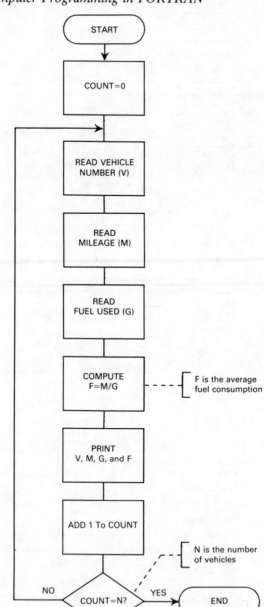

6

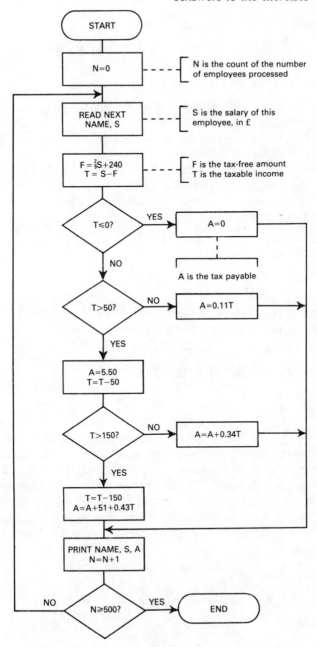

## Chapter 3

1 (a) F9 = 12.46     (b) P = 6.25     (c) ALPHA = 64.0

2 The correct statement is (a):

```
BETA = (A — 3.9) ** 3 * B / 5.6
```

But (d) and (f) are also correct, although the calculations are performed in a different order.

(b) is incorrect: A is subtracted from 3.9

(c) is incorrect: B is cubed

(e) is incorrect: BETA *receives* the value, and must be on the left-hand side of the assignment

(g) is incorrect: A — 3.9 has to be parenthesised

3
```
PROGRAM FORMLA
READ *, D, P, Q
E = (3.479 * D * P ** 2) / (5.67 + Q)
PRINT *, E
END
```

4 `Y = 8 * X ** 3 + 7 * X + 4.3 * X ** 2`

5 The following is termed the 'nested' form of the polynomial. It reduces the total number of arithmetic operations.

```
Y = ((8 * X + 4.3) * X + 7) * X
```

6 (a) 6   (b) 259.0   (c) 19.0   (d) 5.0   (e) 262144   (f) 0.25

## Chapter 5

1 (a) False   (b) False. But such a statement cannot be reached from any other statement, and the compiler should issue an appropriate error message. (c) False (d) True (e) True. The last item in a computed GO TO is an *integer expression* which, in its simplest form, is a variable name. In this case, a true expression is used. Note also that the statement numbers need not all be different and that the comma after the right parenthesis is optional.

2 (a)
```
GO TO (12, 13, 14, 15), (KAJ — 453)
```
  (b)
```
IF (KAJ .EQ. 454) GO TO 12
IF (KAJ .EQ. 455) GO TO 13
IF (KAJ .EQ. 456) GO TO 14
IF (KAJ .EQ. 457) GO TO 15
GO TO error action routine (in case KAJ is out of range)
```

```
(c) IF (KAJ .EQ. 454) THEN
      GO TO 12
    ELSE IF (KAJ .EQ. 455) THEN
      GO TO 13
    ELSE IF (KAJ .EQ. 456) THEN
      GO TO 14
    ELSE IF (KAJ .EQ. 457) THEN
      GO TO 15
    ELSE
      GO TO error action routine
    END IF
```

The preferred approach is probably (a).

```
3 (a) DS .NE. 0 (b) Q .LE. 0 .AND. T9 .EQ. 0
  (c) A4 .GE. 0 .OR. 1 .LE. K .AND. K .LE. 3
  (d) T .NE. S .AND. T ** 2 .EQ. V ** 3
  (e) (C .NE. D .AND. C .NE. E .AND. C .NE. F .AND. C .NE. G)
      .OR.
      (C .EQ. F .AND. D .LT. (E + G))
```

Use more parentheses if you like.

```
4     PROGRAM SEQ
      LOGICAL DONE, OK
      INTEGER OLDX
C
      DONE = .FALSE.
      OK   = .TRUE.
      OLDX = 0
      READ *, NEWX
  10  IF (NEWX .GT. OLDX) THEN
        OLDX = NEWX
        READ *, NEWX
        GO TO 10
      END IF
      IF (NEWX .EQ. -1) THEN
        PRINT *, 'VALID SEQUENCE'
      ELSE
        PRINT *, 'SEQUENCE ERROR'
      END IF
      END
```

(There are many alternative solutions.)

## Chapter 6

1 (a) 10  (b) 5  (c) 4  (d) 9  (e) 0  (f) 3  (g) 5

```
2     PROGRAM DISTS
      DO 10 I = 1, 30
        READ *, X, Y
```

```
          D = SQRT (X * X + Y * Y)
          PRINT *, X, Y, D
   10  CONTINUE
       END

3      PROGRAM MEANS
       INTEGER GROUP, COUNT
C
       TOTAL = 0.0
       NUMBRS = 0
       DO 20 GROUP = 1, 5
          READ *, N
          SUM = 0.0
          DO 10 COUNT = 1, N
             READ *, VALUE
             SUM = SUM + VALUE
   10     CONTINUE
          TOTAL = TOTAL + SUM
          NUMBRS = NUMBRS + N
          PRINT *, 'GROUP:_', GROUP, '_ _ _MEAN:_', SUM/N
   20  CONTINUE
       PRINT *
       PRINT *, 'OVERALL MEAN:_', TOTAL/NUMBRS
       END
```

## Chapter 7

1 (a) (4, 1)   (b) (2, 2)   (c) (1, 3)
  (d) 4   (e) 60   (f) 308

2 `DIMENSION A(6, 17), GIN(0:2, 0:3), D(3) DATE(10, 52, 3)`

3 (a) Second 'I' missing from 'DIMENSION'
  (b) Comma between B(7) and N(16) is omitted

```
4      PROGRAM TRANSP
       DIMENSION MAT (10, 10), MATE (10, 10)
       ...
       DO 20 I = 1, 10
          DO 10 J = 1, 10
             MATE(I,J) = MAT(J,I)**2
   10     CONTINUE
   20  CONTINUE
       ...
       END

5      PROGRAM SQUARES
       INTEGER SQUARE(10, 10), COUNT
C          READ THE SQUARE VALUES
       DO 20 I = 1, 10
```

```
         DO 10 J = 1, 10
    5       READ *, K
            IF (K .LT. 0 .OR. K .GT. 1) THEN
               PRINT *, 'DATA ERROR'
               GO TO 5
            END IF
            SQUARE(I, J) = K
   10    CONTINUE
   20 CONTINUE
C        MAIN LOOP
C        READ AND CHECK CO-ORDINATES
   30 READ *, I
      IF (I .LT. 0) STOP
      IF (I .LT. 1 .OR. I .GT. 10) THEN
        PRINT *, 'OUT OF RANGE'
        GO TO 30
      END IF
   40 READ *, J
      IF (J .LT. 1 .OR. J .GT. 10) THEN
        PRINT *, 'OUT OF RANGE'
        GO TO 40
      END IF
C        COUNT THE SURROUNDING ZEROS
      COUNT = 0
      DO 60 L = I - 1, I + 1
        DO 50 M = J - 1, J + 1
C        WE HAVE TO BE CAREFUL AT THE EDGES AND CORNERS
           IF (L .LT. 1 .OR. L .GT. 10 .OR.
     *         M .LT. 1 .OR. M .GT. 10) GO TO 50
           IF (SQUARE(L, M) .EQ. 0) COUNT = COUNT + 1
   50    CONTINUE
   60 CONTINUE
C        IF SQUARE(I, J) IS ZERO, WE HAVE COUNTED
C        ONE ZERO TOO MANY, AND MUST ADJUST
      IF (SQUARE(I, J) .EQ. 0) COUNT = COUNT - 1
      PRINT *, I, J, COUNT
      GO TO 30
      END
```

## Chapter 8

```
1     PROGRAM ORDER
      CHARACTER * 10 A, B, C
   10 READ *, A, B, C
      IF (A .EQ. '***') STOP
      IF (LLT(A, B)) THEN
        IF (LLT(A, C)) THEN
          IF (LLT(B, C)) THEN
            PRINT *, A, B, C
          ELSE
```

```
            PRINT *, A, C, B
          END IF
        ELSE
          PRINT *, C, A, B
        END IF
      ELSE
        IF (LLT(A, C)) THEN
          PRINT *, B, A, C
        ELSE
          IF (LLT(B, C)) THEN
            PRINT *, B, C, A
          ELSE
            PRINT *, C, B, A
          END IF
        END IF
      END IF
      GO TO 10
      END
```

2 (Basic version)

```
      PROGRAM REVERS
      CHARACTER * 15 WORD, RWORD
   10 READ *, WORD
      IF (WORD .EQ. '***') STOP
      DO 20 I = 1, 15
        RWORD(I:I) = WORD(16-I:16-I)
   20 CONTINUE
      PRINT *
      PRINT *, WORD
      PRINT *, RWORD
      GO TO 10
      END
```

(Improved output – spaces removed)

Delete the three statements of the DO loop, and replace by the following:

```
      J = 1
      RWORD = '_'
      DO 20 I = 1, 15
        K = 16 - I
C         THIS SAVES WRITING '16-I' THREE MORE TIMES
        IF (WORD(K:K) .EQ. '_') GO TO 20
        RWORD(J:J) = WORD(K:K)
        J = J + 1
   20 CONTINUE
```

3
```
      INTEGER WORDS
      CHARACTER LINE(80)
      ...
      WORDS = 0
      DO 10 I = 2, 80
```

```
      IF (LINE(I) .EQ. '_'
     * .OR. LINE(I) .EQ. '.') WORDS = WORDS + 1
 10   CONTINUE
      ...

4     PROGRAM ENCODE
      CHARACTER * 80 PLAIN, CODE
      CHARACTER C
      INTEGER P
      READ *, PLAIN
  5   IF (PLAIN .EQ. '***') STOP
      DO 10 I = 1, 80
C        GET THE NEXT CHARACTER
       C = PLAIN(I:I)
C        IS IT ALPHABETIC?
       IF (LLE('A', C) .AND. LLE(C, 'Z')) THEN
C          IF SO, DETERMINE ITS POSITION IN THE
C          ALPHABET
         P = ICHAR(C) — ICHAR('A') + 1
C          ADD 5 TO GET THE ENCODED CHARACTER'S
C          POSITION, AND CHECK FOR WRAPAROUND
         P = P + 5
         IF (P .GT. 26) P = P — 26
C          WE NOW HAVE TO CHANGE THE NEW
C          POSITION BACK INTO RELATIVE FORM
C          (BY SUBSTRACTING 1), AND THEN GET THE
C          ABSOLUTE INTERNAL CODE BY ADDING THAT FOR
C          'A' BACK AGAIN. WE HAVE ASSUMED THAT ALL
C          THE ALPHABETIC CHARACTERS ARE IN A
C          CONTIGUOUS GROUP WITHIN THE MACHINE'S
C          COLLATING SEQUENCE.
         CODE(I:I) = CHAR(P — 1 + ICHAR('A'))
       ELSE
C          NON-ALPHABETIC CHARACTERS ARE JUST COPIED
         CODE(I:I) = PLAIN(I:I)
       END IF
 10   CONTINUE
      PRINT *
      PRINT *, PLAIN
      PRINT *, CODE
      READ *, PLAIN
      GO TO 5
      END
```

## Chapter 9

3 A statement function is probably the best choice, since the result
  is a single value and the calculation is expressible in a single
  statement:

```
  F(U, V) = U * V / (U + V)
```

```
4 FUNCTION KOMPAR (I, J)
  IF (I .LT. J) THEN
    KOMPAR = -1
  ELSE IF ( I .EQ. J) THEN
    KOMPAR = 0
  ELSE
    KOMPAR = 1
  END IF
  END
```

This is interesting because it is very straightforward when dealing with integers, but if I and J were reals, we should need to be a little more careful. The problem is one of deciding when two floating-point quantities are 'equal'. The difference between two real values, calculated by different instruction sequences but representing the same value, may not, because of the nature of floating-point arithmetic, be exactly zero. The difference will be small, but may be sufficient to invalidate a test for zero – or equality. We shall be obliged to decide what is a small enough difference, for our purpose, that we may *regard* it as zero. If we were to choose a difference between the arguments of, say, $1 \times 10^{-6}$ we could write a function like this:

```
FUNCTION KOMPAR(I, J)
REAL I, J
PARAMETER (TOL = 1.0E-6)
IF (ABS(I - J) .LE. TOL) THEN
  KOMPAR = 0
ELSE IF ((I - J) .LT. -TOL) THEN
  KOMPAR = -1
ELSE
  KOMPAR = 1
END IF
END
```

```
5 CHARACTER * 6 FUNCTION GET (S, I, T)
  CHARACTER * 6 S(*), T
  K = (I - 1)/6
  L = I - 6 * K
  T = '_ _ _ _ _ _'
  T(1:1) = S(K+1) (L:L)
  GET = T
  END
```

*Note:* this function has a 'side effect', in that it gives a value to T as well as returning a value in the usual manner. Generally speaking, this is not considered good practice, but you will meet examples such as that given here.

6 (a) False   (b) True   (c) False   (d) False – it appears in an
  EXTERNAL statement in the *calling* program


# Chapter 10

```
1      SUBROUTINE WTAKE
       COMMON WEEK(7), TAKE
       TAKE = 0.0
       DO 10 I = 1, 7
         TAKE = TAKE + WEEK(I)
    10 CONTINUE
       RETURN
C          'RETURN' MAY BE OMITTED, SINCE,
C          IN THIS PROGRAM, THE 'END' STATEMENT
C          SERVES THE SAME PURPOSE
       END

2      SUBROUTINE FIDDLE (A, B)
       REAL NEWX
    10 READ *, X
       IF (X .LT. 0.0) RETURN
C        THIS 'RETURN' IS NECESSARY, SINCE IT IS THE
C        ONLY EXIT FROM THE SUBROUTINE
       NEWX = A * X + B
       PRINT *, X, NEWX
       GO TO 10
       END

3      PROGRAM SCAN
       CHARACTER LINE*80(100)
C          THIS IS THE DRIVING ROUTINE
       DO 10 I = 1, 5
         READ *, LINE(I)
    10 CONTINUE
       LINE(6) = '*'
       CALL QUERY(LINE, NUM)
       PRINT *, 'THERE ARE_', NUM, '_QUESTIONS.'
       END
       SUBROUTINE QUERY(TEXT, N)
       CHARACTER TEXT*80(*)
C          THE COUNT OF THE NUMBER OF QUESTION
C          MARKS IS DEVELOPED IN N
       N = 0
       I = 1
    10 IF (TEXT(I) (1:1) .EQ. '*') RETURN
       DO 20 J = 1, 80
C          SCAN ONE LINE, LOOKING FOR '?'
         IF (TEXT(I) (J:J) .EQ. '?') N = N + 1
    20 CONTINUE
```

```
C          MOVE TO THE NEXT LINE
      I = I + 1
      GO TO 10
      END

4     SUBROUTINE BUF(CH)
      CHARACTER CH, STRING*6(20)
      COMMON /A/ NEXT, /B/ STRING
C
      IF (NEXT .GT. 120) THEN
        DO 10 I = 1, 20
          PRINT *, STRING(I)
   20   CONTINUE
        NEXT = 1
      END IF
C          NOW WE HAVE TO DETERMINE THE WORD
C          OF STRING IN WHICH THE NEXT
C          CHARACTER LIES, AND ITS POSITION
C          WITHIN THAT WORD. I AND J ARE
C          HERE USED FOR WORD AND POSITION,
C          RESPECTIVELY. ( 'WORD' MEANS 'ARRAY
C          ELEMENT')
      I = (NEXT - 1) / 6 + 1
      J = NEXT - (I - 1) * 6
      STRING(I) (J:J) = CH
      NEXT = NEXT + 1
      END
```

## Chapter 11

```
1         PROGRAM TABLE
          INTEGER THETA
          WRITE(6, 100)
   100    FORMAT ('1', 16X, 'R', 8X, 'THETA', 6X, 'X', 9X,
                 'Y')
          DO 10 THETA = 0, 360, 10
            ANGLE = 0.0174533 * THETA
C            WE HAD TO DO THAT, BECAUSE SIN AND COS LIKE
C            THEIR ARGUMENTS IN RADIANS, NOT DEGREES
            R = 2 * COS (ANGLE)
C            NOW CALL THE CONVERSION ROUTINE
            CALL RTOC (R, ANGLE, X, Y)
            WRITE (6, 200) R, THETA, X, Y
   200      FORMAT (11X, E13.6, 17, 2F10.4)
   10     CONTINUE
          END
          SUBROUTINE RTOC (R, ANGLE, X, Y)
          X = R * COS (ANGLE)
          Y = R * SIN (ANGLE)
          END
```

```
2       ...
        LOGICAL A, B, NONEQ
        ...
        NONEQ = A .AND. .NOT. B .OR. B .AND. .NOT. A
        WRITE (6, 100) A, B, NONEQ
 100    FORMAT (1X, 'A_=_', L2, '_ _B_=_', L2,
     *               '_ _NONEQUIVALENT:_ _', L2)
        ...


3       PROGRAM SUNNY
        CHARACTER * 9 DAY, WKDAY, NOT * 3
        INTEGER D
        LOGICAL S
 10     READ (5, 100) D, S
 100    FORMAT (I1, L1)
        IF (D .GT. 7) STOP
        WKDAY = DAY (D)
        IF (WKDAY .EQ. '*********') THEN
          PRINT *, 'DATA ERROR'
          GO TO 10
        END IF
        IF (S) THEN
          NOT = '_ _ _'
        ELSE
          NOT = 'NOT'
        END IF
        WRITE (6, 200) WKDAY, NOT
 200    FORMAT (1X, 'IT_IS_', A9, '_AND_THE_SUN_IS_',
     *          A3, '_SHINING')
        GO TO 10
        END
        CHARACTER * 9 FUNCTION DAY (N)
        IF (N .LT. 1 .OR. N .GT. 7) THEN
          DAY = '*********'
          RETURN
        ELSE
          GO TO (10, 20, 30, 40, 50, 60, 70), N
 10       DAY = 'SUNDAY'
          RETURN
 20       DAY = 'MONDAY'
          RETURN
 30       DAY = 'TUESDAY'
          RETURN
 40       DAY = 'WEDNESDAY'
          RETURN
 50       DAY = 'THURSDAY'
          RETURN
 60       DAY = 'FRIDAY'
          RETURN
 70       DAY = 'SATURDAY'
```

```
        RETURN
      END IF
      END
```

This is really pretty awful, and so are the alternatives in your present state of knowledge. In Chapter 13 you will find a description of the DATA statement, which enables us to do things a bit more neatly:

```
      CHARACTER * 9 FUNCTION DAY (N)
      CHARACTER * 9 DAYS (7)
      SAVE DAYS
      DATA (DAYS(I), I = 1, 7) / 'SUNDAY', 'MONDAY',
    *        'TUESDAY',   'WEDNESDAY',   'THURSDAY',
             'FRIDAY',
    *        'SATURDAY' /
C     THIS HAS SET UP AN ARRAY CONTAINING THE
C     NAMES OF THE DAYS OF THE WEEK
      IF (N .LT. 1 .OR. N .GT. 7) THEN
        DAY = '*********'
      ELSE
        DAY = DAYS (N)
      END IF
      END
```

```
4       WRITE (6, 100) PAGNO AREA
  100   FORMAT ('1', 27X, 'LIST_OF_SUSPECTED_PERSONS',
    *          ////// 70X, 'PAGE:', I5,
    *          ////// 26X, A20, '_REGION')
```

5 (a) Probably false, since the first character of the 132 sent to the printer will be 'stolen' for carriage control

  (b) False   (c) True   (d) False   (e) True – the effect is to skip the next input record   (f) False   (g) False

# Chapter 12

```
1       PROGRAM SPLIT
        CHARACTER * 122 STRING
        OPEN (7, FILE = 'MASTER', STATUS = 'OLD',
    *             ERR = 99999)
        OPEN (8, FILE = 'TEMP1', STATUS = 'NEW',
    *             ERR = 99998)
        OPEN (9, FILE = 'TEMP2', STATUS = 'NEW',
    *             ERR = 99997)
   10   READ (7, 100, END = 888) N, STRING
  100   FORMAT (I6, A)
        IF (N .GE. 0) THEN
```

```
          WRITE (9, 100) N, STRING
        ELSE
          WRITE (8, 100) N, STRING
        END IF
        GO TO 10
  888   END FILE 8
        END FILE 9
        CLOSE (7)
        CLOSE (8)
        CLOSE (9)
        STOP
99997 PRINT *, 'ERROR IN OPENING TEMP2'
        STOP
99998 PRINT *, 'ERROR IN OPENING TEMP1'
        STOP
99999 PRINT *, 'ERROR IN OPENING MASTER'
        END

2       PROGRAM SPREAD
        CHARACTER * 122 STRING
        OPEN (8, FILE = 'TEMP1', STATUS = 'OLD',
     *             ERR = 998)
        OPEN (10, FILE = 'D1', STATUS = 'NEW',
     *              ERR = 999, ACCESS = 'DIRECT',
     *              RECL = 128)
  10  READ (8, 100, END = 888) N, STRING
  100 FORMAT (I6, A)
        IF (N .LT. 1 .OR. N .GT. 9999) THEN
          WRITE (6, 200) N, STRING
  200     FORMAT (1X, I6, 1X, A)
        ELSE
          WRITE (10, REC = N) N, STRING
        END IF
        GO TO 10
  888 CLOSE (8)
        CLOSE (10)
        STOP
  998 PRINT *, 'ERROR IN OPENING TEMP1'
        STOP
  999 PRINT *, 'ERROR IN OPENING D1'
        END
```

# Appendix A

## Table of intrinsic functions

| Purpose | Definition | Number of arguments | Generic name | Specific name | Type of argument | Type of result |
|---------|-----------|--------------------|--------------|---------------|-----------------|----------------|
| Type conversion | To integer | 1 | INT | INT | real | integer |
| | | | | IDINT | double | integer |
| | | | | IFIX | real | integer |
| | | | | INT | complex | integer |
| | To real | 1 | REAL | REAL | integer | real |
| | | | | | complex | real |
| | | | | FLOAT | integer | real |
| | | | | SNGL | double | real |
| | To double precision | 1 | DBLE | DBLE | integer | double |
| | | | | | real | double |
| | | | | | complex | double |
| | To complex | 1 or 2 | CMPLX | CMPLX | integer | complex |
| | | | | | real | complex |
| | | | | | double | complex |

| Purpose | Definition | Number of arguments | Generic name | Specific name | Type of argument | Type of result |
|---|---|---|---|---|---|---|
| | Character to integer | 1 | | ICHAR | character | integer |
| | Integer to character | 1 | | CHAR | integer | character |
| Truncation | REAL(INT(x)) DBLE(INT(x)) | 1 | AINT | AINT DINT | real double | real double |
| Nearest whole number | See note 1 | 1 | ANINT | ANINT DNINT | real double | real double |
| Nearest integer | See note 2 | 1 | NINT | NINT IDNINT | real double | integer integer |
| Absolute value | SQRT(x**2) See note 3 | 1 | ABS | ABS IABS DABS CABS | real integer double complex | real integer double real |
| Remainder after division | See note 4 | 2 | MOD | MOD AMOD DMOD | integer real double | integer real double |
| Transfer of sign | See note 5 | 2 | SIGN | SIGN ISIGN DSIGN | real integer double | real integer double |
| Positive difference | x1–x2 if x1 > x2 otherwise, 0 | 2 | DIM | DIM IDIM DDIM | real integer double | real integer double |

| Purpose | Definition | Number of arguments | Generic name | Specific name | Type of argument | Type of result |
|---|---|---|---|---|---|---|
| Double-precision product | x1 * x2 | 2 | | DPROD | real | double |
| Find largest value | See note 6 | more than 1 | MAX | MAX0 AMAX1 DMAX1 | integer real double | integer real double |
| Find smallest value | See note 6 | more than 1 | MIN | MIN0 AMIN1 DMIN1 | integer real double | integer real double |
| Determine length of character entity | Number of characters | 1 | | LEN | character | integer |
| Index of a substring | Location of substring x2 in string x1 | 2 | | INDEX | character | integer |
| Square root | x ** 0.5 | 1 | SQRT | SQRT DSQRT CSQRT | real double complex | real double complex |
| Exponential | e ** x | 1 | EXP | EXP DEXP CEXP | real double complex | real double complex |

| Purpose | Definition | Number of arguments | Generic name | Specific name | Type of argument | Type of result |
|---|---|---|---|---|---|---|
| Natural logarithm | $\log_e x$ | 1 | LOG | ALOG | real | real |
| | | | | DLOG | double | double |
| | | | | CLOG | complex | complex |
| Common logarithm | $\log_{10} x$ | 1 | LOG10 | ALOG10 | real | real |
| | | | | DLOG10 | double | double |
| Sine | $\sin x$ | 1 | SIN | SIN | real | real |
| | | | | DSIN | double | double |
| | | | | CSIN | complex | complex |
| Cosine | $\cos x$ | 1 | COS | COS | real | real |
| | | | | DCOS | double | double |
| | | | | CCOS | complex | complex |
| Tangent | $\tan x$ | 1 | TAN | TAN | real | real |
| | | | | DTAN | double | double |
| Arcsine | $\sin^{-1} x$ | 1 | ASIN | ASIN | real | real |
| | | | | DASIN | double | double |
| Arccosine | $\cos^{-1} x$ | 1 | ACOS | ACOS | real | real |
| | | | | DACOS | double | double |
| Arctangent | $\tan^{-1} x$ | 1 | ATAN | ATAN | real | real |
| | | | | DATAN | double | double |
| | $\tan^{-1} (x1/x2)$ See note 7 | 2 | ATAN2 | ATAN2 | real | real |
| | | | | DATAN2 | double | double |

| Purpose | Definition | Number of arguments | Generic name | Specific name | Type of argument | Type of result |
|---|---|---|---|---|---|---|
| Hyperbolic sine | sinh x | 1 | SINH | SINH<br>DSINH | real<br>double | real<br>double |
| Hyperbolic cosine | cosh x | 1 | COSH | COSH<br>DCOSH | real<br>double | real<br>double |
| Hyperbolic tangent | tanh x | 1 | TANH | TANH<br>DTANH | real<br>double | real<br>double |
| Lexical comparisons | less than | 2 | | LLT | character | logical |
| | less than or equal to | 2 | | LLE | character | logical |
| | greater than or equal to | 2 | | LGE | character | logical |
| | greater than | 2 | | LGT | character | logical |
| Extract imaginary part of complex number | Returns B, where X = A + iB | 1 | | AIMAG | complex | real |
| Complex conjugate | A − iB, where X = A + iB | 1 | | CONJG | complex | complex |

## Notes

1 REAL (INT $(x + 0.5)$) or DBLE (INT $(x + 0.5)$) if $x \geqslant 0$
  REAL (INT $(x - 0.5)$) or DBLE (INT $(x - 0.5)$) if $x < 0$
2 INT $(x + 0.5)$ if $x \geqslant 0$
  INT $(x - 0.5)$ if $x < 0$
3 If x is the complex quantity A + *i*B,

```
ABS (X) = SQRT (A**2 + B**2)
```

4 Both arguments of MOD must be of the same type. The result, also
  of that type, is the remainder when the first argument, x1, is
  divided by the second, x2. Specifically, this means that:

```
MOD (X1, X2) = X1 - (INT (X1/X2) * X2)
AMOD (X1, X2) = REAL (X1 - (INT (X1/X2) * X2))
DMOD (X1, X2) = DBLE (X1 - (INT (X1/X2) * X2))
```

  x2 must be non-zero.
5 ABS $(x1)$ if $x2 \geqslant 0$, $-$ABS $(x1)$ if $x2 < 0$.
6 There are also specific functions for finding maximum and
  minimum values that produce a result of a type differing from
  that of the arguments. But the whole set of specific names is so
  confusing that it is probably better to stick to the generic forms
  MAX and MIN, together with – if necessary – the appropriate type
  conversion generic. For example:

```
REAL (MAX (I, J, K, L, M))
DBLE (MIN (P, Q, R, S))
INT (MIN (A, B, C, D))
```

7 The tangent of an angle is, of course, the ratio of the lengths of
  two sides of a right-angled triangle. Given the two lengths, x1 and
  x2, we can either use ATAN2 $(x1, x2)$ or ATAN $(x1/x2)$. In either
  case, we get the angle (in radians) whose tangent is x1/x2.

# Appendix B

## FORTRAN 77 and FORTRAN 66

FORTRAN is a living language, changed at intervals as defined by the American National Standards Institute (ANSI). FORTRAN 77 is the latest version, but already thought is being given to the changes needed at the next revision.

Even so, FORTRAN 77 does not seem to be so widely available as one might have hoped, considering the time that has elapsed since the new standard was introduced. For this reason, a brief summary of the more important differences between FORTRAN 77 and its immediate predecessor, often called FORTRAN 66, is given here.

In FORTRAN 66:

1 The PROGRAM statement is invalid.
2 REAL and INTEGER entities may not be mixed in an arithmetic expression. The intrinsic functions FLOAT and IFIX (or INT) can be used for integer-to-real conversion, and vice versa.

> A + 3 * B must be written as A + 3.0 * B
> A + I * B should be A + FLOAT(I) * B

3 A ** B ** C is not acceptable; it must be made unambiguous by the use of parentheses.
4 READ * and PRINT are not available, and nor are READ (*, . . .) . . . and WRITE (*, . . .) . . . . All READ and WRITE statements must be of the form

READ $(u, f)$ ... $\Big\rvert$ formatted, or READ $(u)$ ... $\Big\rvert$ unformatted
WRITE $(u, f)$ ... $\Big\rvert$ WRITE $(u)$ ...

where $u$ is the device number and $f$ the statement number of a FORMAT statement; $f$ may also be the name of an array that holds a format list in character form.

5 All comments must start with a 'c' in column 1.

6 The block IF features (IF . . . THEN, ELSE, ELSE IF and END IF) are not available. Only the logical and arithmetic IF statements may be used.

7 The action taken if the selector of a computed GO TO is out of range is not defined.

8 There are comparatively severe DO loop restrictions:
   (a) DO parameters must be *integer* constants, or variables; more complicated expressions are not allowed.
   (b) Regardless of the values of the parameters – even if the initial value exceeds that of the limit – the statements in the range of the DO are executed at least once.
   (c) There may *not* be a comma after the label following 'DO'.
   (d) The values of the parameters may not be negative.

9 Arrays may have at most three dimensions, and each subscript has a lower bound of 1. The DIMENSION statement thus needs only to give the upper bound for each dimension. For example,

```
DIMENSION, A(100, B(10, 10), C(10, 5, 2)
```

10 The number following PAUSE or STOP must be an octal value in the range 0 to 77777 (no digit to exceed 7).

11 There is no CHARACTER type, and hence no CHARACTER operations. Nevertheless, character strings can be stored in real and integer variables by using the A format on input. See your FORTRAN 66 manual for details.

12 Character constants are often expressed in exactly the same way as in FORTRAN 77, using quotes to enclose the character string. This is not, however, the method specified in the Standard, which requires the use of *Hollerith constants*, of which the following are typical examples:

```
11HAPPLE_GREEN
10HFORTRAN_77
18HTHAT'S_ALL_FOLKS!
```

(Once again, the underline is used to show the presence of a space.) Each Hollerith constant consists of the value of the constant (i.e. the string of characters) preceded by the letter 'H', which is in turn preceded by a count of the number of characters in the string. The FORTRAN 77 equivalents of the above example are:

'APPLE_GREEN', 'FORTRAN_77' and 'THAT'S_ALL_FOLKS!'

13　FORTRAN 66 does not support generic functions. There are intrinsic functions (which may not be used as arguments of other functions, so the INTRINSIC statement is not needed) and 'basic external functions' covering most normal needs.

14　Functions must have at least one argument.

15　The use of '*' for dimensioning arrays passed as arguments is not supported.

16　The T, TL, TR, BZ, BN, colon, I$w.d$, E$w.d$E$e$, SP and SS format specifications are not available.

17　There are no OPEN or CLOSE statements.

18　The implied DO loop may not be used for DATA initialisation.

19　The IMPLICIT statement is not (officially) available.

20　There is no SAVE statement.

# Index

# Index

## COMPUTER PROGRAMMING
## IN BASIC

## L. R. CARTER and E. HUZAN

BASIC (Beginners All-purpose Symbolic Instruction Code) is a widely used programming language in education, commerce and industry, particularly for mini- and microcomputers, and by the hobbyist.

A knowledge of BASIC provides a useful introduction to computer programming and allows effective practical applications to be developed on many systems.

This book provides a practical grounding in BASIC. An elementary description of the functions of a computer is followed by an explanation of the purpose of system commands for running BASIC programs. There are also chapters on program development and testing. Exercises are provided throughout and answers to problems and suggested programs are given in appendices. The final chapter of the book illustrates the use of BASIC for a range of simple mathematical, scientific and business applications.

TEACH YOURSELF BOOKS

# COMPUTER PROGRAMMING IN COBOL

## MELINDA FISHER

COBOL (COmmon Business Oriented Language) is the computer language which is most widely used in business and commerce, for invoicing, stock control, payroll and management information systems, on both microcomputer and mainframe installations.

This book looks first at the basic concepts of computers and computer programming before examining the language, logic design and special features of COBOL. Starting from first principles, the book systematically introduces and explains the main COBOL facilities, language statements and relevant syntax. Thus the reader progresses in easy stages from data description and manipulation, through sequence control and handling sequential files and tables, to producing printed reports and indexing. Sample programs illustrate the everyday application of COBOL facilities and a fully documented example shows how a tested, working program is developed from an initial specification. Exercises (with answers) are provided throughout.

TEACH YOURSELF BOOKS

# COMPUTER PROGRAMMING
# IN PASCAL

## DAVID LIGHTFOOT

Pascal is a general-purpose computer language which has become popular for its compact yet powerful facilities on a wide variety of microcomputers (including personal computers) and mainframe systems alike.

The simple nature of Pascal makes for clearly structured programming giving rise to programs which are easy to read, modify and show to be correct. As such, it is also one of the easier computer languages to learn.

This book provides a sound introduction to Pascal in its standard (BSI) and UCSD implementations. David Lightfoot first describes its general rules and standard types. Then, with the aid of many examples and illustrations, he gives a step-by-step explanation of Pascal statements and syntax – including branching, looping and dealing with sequential files – and practical advice on program design. Exercises (with answers) are included to give a thorough grounding in programming for a wide range of applications, while a graded selection of sample programs highlights the flexibility offered by Pascal.

TEACH YOURSELF BOOKS

# MICROELECTRONICS AND MICROCOMPUTERS

## L. R. CARTER and E. HUZAN

Microelectronic devices and microcomputers are increasingly used for a wide range of applications because of their compactness, low cost and versatility. These applications require a knowledge of the devices available and how they may be linked, and the user must also be aware of the problems and procedure associated with the analysis, programming and running of the application.

This book provides an introduction to microelectronic devices, number systems and logic circuits, microcomputer structure and functions, interfacing and data communications, programming and system development. Applications include those dealing with aspects of instrumentation, industry, travel, leisure, education and office use.

The book is suitable for the first-time business or scientific user, and the engineer and scientist using microprocessors for recording measurements and controlling processes. The hobbyist, home user and student of microcomputers will find this book useful as background reading for project work.

TEACH YOURSELF BOOKS